The Association Guide to Going Global

The Association Guide to Going Global

New Strategies for a Changing Economic Landscape

Steven M. Worth

WILEY
John Wiley & Sons, Inc.

Published by John Wiley & Sons, Inc., Hoboken, New Jersey.
Published simultaneously in Canada.

Library of Congress Cataloging-in-Publication Data:

Worth, Steven M.
The association guide to going global : new strategies for a changing economic landscape/ Steven M. Worth.
p. cm.
Includes index.
ISBN 978-0-470-58789-8 (cloth)
1. Trade associations. 2. Associations, institutions, etc.
3. International business enterprises. 4. Globalization. I. Title.
HD2421.W68 2010
658'.049—dc22

2010006832

Printed in the United States of America

10 9 8 7 6 5 4 3 2 1

This book is dedicated to the volunteer leadership and professional staff who guided and made the tough decisions described in this book. The wisdom of their decisions has since shown through, but at the time they were made it was not at all clear that this was the right course of action. Their courage marks them as trailblazers. They not only built solid foundations for the global growth of their organizations; they set an example of leadership from which we can all learn.

Contents

Foreword

In the non-profit world of associations and philanthropic organizations, globalization is a condition that was largely unknown only a decade ago. It was less than ten years ago that the American Society of Association Executives (ASAE) conducted a survey of the major issues and concerns of senior association executives. Globalization and worldwide activities were not a significant concern for the majority of respondents! Yet, the process of globalization is not new. It has been taking place for a long time, particularly in the highly competitive for-profit world. For much of the nonprofit sector, however, globalization has been little more than a vague concept, or worse, just an overused and inapplicable cliché. Times have changed!

Today, even in the world of nonprofit associations and philanthropic organizations, globalization is becoming one of the highest priorities, fueled by the example of the increasingly competitive for-profit world economy, where downsizing and offshoring in the United States (and elsewhere) have become commonplace. Globalization has accelerated even faster over the past couple of years with the substantial economic decline in the United States and elsewhere. Suddenly, large and small nonprofits are seeking information and experience for expanding their members, goods, and services beyond the borders of their historic local, regional, and national U.S. area of operations. Suddenly, globalization is real and tangible.

But there are some important questions to be asked and more important answers that are needed. For example, just what is globalization? How is globalization defined and measured? Is globalization exporting some publications outside the United States? Is globalization having a separate category of membership for persons residing outside the United States? Does an office outside the United States qualify a nonprofit as a global organization?

Beyond definition, there are key nonprofit organization issues of mission and goals. Does globalization support or compete with my organization's mission and goals? Should my organization aspire to be global, and if so, how do we get there? And what if my organization has been operating outside the United States—is there anything more to be learned?

Beyond these important issues are other considerations: the planning and operational issues—the structural issues. What are the organizational planning and implementation options for globalization? Which options best fit the mission and goals of my organization? What has been the experience of those organizations that have been involved in global operations for years?

Just how can one consider and translate the globalization cliché to fit a specific nonprofit organization? Or does one size fit all?

Steven Worth's book brings together an amazing range of global experience in the nonprofit sector together with wide-ranging case studies and specific globalization examples. For the first time, as far as I am aware, executives and leaders in the nonprofit world have a comprehensive and focused resource about globalization that is specifically tailored to the nonprofit sector. It's a resource that is action oriented, tailored to support the debate, decision making, and strategic and operational planning necessary for successful globalization by nonprofit organizations that wish to embark on that journey. For nonprofits already conducting worldwide operations, the book is full of case studies and shared experience that will help strengthen existing global activities.

From all appearances, globalization will be around for a long time to come. It promises to become a common part of our vocabulary, and our business planning and operations, for as far forward as we can see. Steve Worth's experience and book provide the nonprofit sector with an invaluable resource to deal with the new, global way of our seeing and operating in our world.

Virgil R. Carter, Executive Director (retired)
American Society of Mechanical Engineers (ASME)

Introduction

You know you are global when:

- Your organization feels as "at home" in any one culture or in any one part of the globe as in another.
- Your customers and stakeholders view your organization as "a local organization" wherever they and you may be in the world.
- Your organization is able to sift through local trends and ways of doing things to identify what has potential on a global scale, and is able to apply global trends and strategies effectively at the local level everywhere in the world.
- As markets rise and fall, you are able to shift resources fluently from one to another so that your overall organization continues to thrive and produce intellectual property that is wanted and needed throughout the world.

In other words, being global assures that you act as and are perceived to be a citizen in every community of the world, that you are able to bring resources to bear when and where there are opportunities, and that you are adept at recognizing and addressing trends in customer needs and wants on a local as well as a global scale. Isn't this the formula for any successful organization?

These qualities most certainly characterize successful organizations at the local or national level; so, in one regard, globalization is mostly a matter of scope—but what scope it is! When the world's cultural, ethnic, linguistic, legal, and political differences are all thrown together on one playing board we have a game with moving parts that is more complex than playing three-dimensional chess. Then, just to make it interesting, throw into the mix the differences in financial, educational, and technological means from one country to another—not to mention the challenges of distance and sheer geographical differences—and you have a very intimidating picture, indeed!

Is anyone able to win at such a complex game? Yes, every day. In fact these are the organizations that touch every aspect of our lives, from the products we use and consume to the health care treatment we receive. The global flow of products and services and the ideas they contain are all the result of organizations that have been conceived to satisfy our wants and needs. If they are not global themselves, they are linked in to organizations that are.

The global sharing of ideas and competition among people and organizations on a global scale can and do result in discoveries—including new cures for old diseases, and better products at less cost. Few energy sources are greater than those that can successfully harness the minds and creativity of the six billion human souls that inhabit our planet—or a portion thereof! But of course, globalization is not all sunshine and roses. If your particular product or service is not among the best, then globalization can be a painful experience—as news about plant closings and business failures tell us every day. So the trek toward becoming a global organization can be seen to be as much defensive as it is progressive. If your organization does not find and fill its global niche, then the chances are good that someone else, somewhere else will!

Textbooks typically point out that there are three types of transnational organizations:

1. "International" organizations that operate across national boundaries because they buy or sell internationally, have international meetings or alliances, and serve stakeholders or members from other countries. In international organizations, there is little customization of goods and services for global customers, and the organization's

business and governance structures are highly concentrated on the domestic market. Customers, whether local or global, are treated the same.

2. "Multinational" organizations that have a sustainable and ongoing presence in more than one national market simultaneously. Goods and services may often be customized for a country-by-country market, and the operational and governance structures may be distributed among and within these targeted countries. Local customers, regardless of location, are the priority, but global customers outside of these markets may be supported only with difficulty.
3. "Global" organizations that fulfill all four of the characteristics noted at the beginning of the introduction. Goods and services allow for major customization. The business and governance structures are highly networked and distributed. Customers are supported both locally and globally.

Unless you have merged your organization into another to become global instantaneously, for most, becoming global is a gradual, step-by-step process in which a domestic organization becomes international, then multinational, then global. It is a time-consuming, difficult process, but it is a challenge that this generation cannot refuse. Globalization is something this generation and every generation after us will have to incorporate into their education, mind-set, and day-to-day living. It is the trend that most defines our times. Those people and organizations that adapt to it best are the ones that will reap the most rewards.

Organizations based in smaller countries with advanced economies have a special advantage in that they are used to dealing with foreign languages and cultures. Cross-border transactions are a daily occurrence for them. It is no wonder then that managers from the Netherlands who seem to be multilingual at birth are in much demand as managers in global organizations.

The old joke, told mostly by Europeans, that a person who speaks three languages is called trilingual, a person who speaks two languages is called bilingual, and a person who speaks one language is called, you guessed it—an American—contains a sharp bit of truth. When one is born on a continent where well over 300 million people speak the same language and that constitutes the largest economic market in the world, it is easy to be parochial without seeming to be under-educated! Nevertheless, for this reason, Americans are at a disadvantage when it comes to understanding and operating successfully in a global environment. It is for this reason that this book focuses particularly on the challenges faced by U.S. managers as they grapple with globalization.

This book, of course, also focuses on associations. While the management tactics and strategies that are discussed here could be and are applied to all sorts of organizations, associations have a particularly important role in globalization, for two reasons. First, associations—and that includes trade associations and professional societies (and other individual membership organizations) as well as chambers of commerce—have played a particularly important role by providing the networking contacts and market intelligence small and medium-size enterprises (SMEs) have needed in order to expand as rapidly as they have into global markets. As is discussed in the first chapter, SMEs have been the surprise winners in globalization, snatching the prize out from under the noses of the giant but lumbering multinational companies that have not been as nimble in taking advantage of new opportunities in new markets, and associations have a lot to do with this. The second reason why associations deserve special attention is the critical role they can and do play in addressing issues of social responsibility that all too often fall through the cracks between the secular interests of national governments and for profit undertakings. To a large extent, associations are just now coming into their own, and their effectiveness in this current and future role will be largely defined by how well they have learned to navigate in a global environment.

How the Book Is Organized

This book is divided into eight chapters that correspond to those issues or problem areas that naturally crop up whenever a conversation turns to globalization. While sticking to the facts, I also attempt to use personal anecdotes and stories to liven up what some textbooks have turned into a dry topic. Globalization deserves better. It is about flesh and blood, dreams that have been dashed, as well as dreams that have resulted in fabulous success. More importantly, it is about a topic that affects all of us. It defines our time, and how we cope with it will determine the quality of our future.

Here is how we will take this journey:

Chapter 1: Why Go Global?

This chapter addresses the trends, opportunities and threats of globalization for associations and how successful associations have responded. It also addresses the emerging opportunities that are unique to the association community and what associations need to do to ready themselves for these roles.

Chapter 2: Common Problems in the Global Arena

There is enough of a track record now to be able to learn from the successes and failures of others. This chapter attempts to catalog the lessons that have been learned so that others may build on them.

Chapter 3: The Structure of the Globalized Association

This chapter addresses the different stages in cross border transactions from international to multinational to global. It also addresses the different structures that have found to be suitable for organizations of varying means and missions. There are as many variations in globalization as there are organizations, but there are some broad models and lessons that have been learned that might serve to structure and inspire others that have faced or are facing similar challenges.

Chapter 4: Funding and Financing

Even the most altruistic associations need funding to fuel global operations. This chapter focuses on those considerations and how successful associations have addressed them.

Chapter 5: Language and Culture

These are the most obvious differences among international markets, yet language and cultural differences continue to be stumbling blocks for individuals and organizations operating across national borders.

This chapter discusses some of the gaffes that can happen and how successful managers avoid making them!

Chapter 6: Endeavors in Specific Countries

This chapter discusses the differences between lesser-developed, developing, and developed economies and how each pose a different set of challenges and opportunities. It also discusses BEMs (big emerging markets) and the BRIC countries (Brazil, Russia, India, and China) and the do's and don'ts of entering those markets.

Chapter 7: Successes and Failures

This chapter discusses successful strategies and models that have been used by associations that have expanded globally.

Chapter 8: Final Thoughts on Truly Becoming "Global"

This chapter discusses the nature of the globalization challenge for association managers and why it is a challenge that no manager can ignore.

Chapter 1

Why Go Global?

Associations are consensus-driven organizations. In this regard, this chapter is designed to provide association leaders the facts and the rationale they need to launch their organizations into a discussion about globalization and how it applies to them. This chapter addresses the following:

- How globalization defines the economic, social, commercial, technological, and political trends of our time.
- How globalization is both a challenge and an opportunity to associations facing declining membership.
- How globalization represents market forces that, if followed, will naturally lead organizations into the global arena.
- The popular belief that globalization is only for large, wealthy organizations.
- Why globalization is ideally suited to the missions of most associations.
- What arguments will support your decision to go global.

- Why now is the right time for associations to play a greater role on the world stage.

Long-Term Implication of Current Trends

This discussion touches on a number of daily trends and concerns that have very long-term implications for us all—individually, organizationally, and nationally. Some of these trends are rising energy costs, increased concern about our carbon footprints, personal quality of life concerns, and generational differences in technology comfort levels.

Certainly, fuel costs and pollution consciousness are having and will continue to have a major impact on consumption and commuting patterns in the United States. In early 2009, the price of a gallon of gasoline in Germany and Turkey—two countries that pay the most for their automobile fuel—was US$11.90. But even outside of these two countries, much of the rest of the world pays at least close to double what Americans currently pay at the pump. Can U.S. price rises be far behind? So as Americans contemplate the near-term possibility of $8-a-gallon gasoline prices, as well as the impact of greenhouse gases (current record-breaking temperatures and bizarre weather patterns are just a foretaste of more to come!), can changing consumer patterns and lifestyle changes be far behind?

Discussion of a shorter workweek that has become more common in the United States has been the subject of passionate debate in France for many years. France currently has a legally mandated 35-hour workweek (along with a minimum of six weeks' guaranteed vacation time a year) that was designed to address quality-of-life issues and to combat the perceived "race to the bottom" effects of globalization.

But, as Thomas Friedman, author of *The World Is Flat*, pointed out, *although the French were trying to create a 35-hour workweek, the Indians were busy figuring out how to fit 35 hours into a single workday!*

Friedman's comments proved to be prophetic during a conversation I had with a small business owner in France who prides himself on his concern with quality-of-life issues. Pierre is against what he sees as brutal American-style capitalism and therefore against any rollback of these hard-earned French workers' rights. I asked Pierre how his own business was doing. Without skipping a beat, he responded happily that his business was doing just fine since he sent most of his production to an affiliate operation in China.

The added dimension in all of these concerns is global. As U.S. fuel prices go up and we turn more corn into ethanol, riots are taking place in Egyptian cities over the rising costs of bread. And as we rationalize how easy it is to telecommute, we come to the same conclusion that professionals in India have reached—telecommuting works! Who knows or cares whether the person on the other end of the fax, email, or telephone call is in India as long as the work gets done? If you don't think this global dimension affects us all, then you need to think again.

Talent has become a commodity to be bought and sold over the Internet. It used to be that Westerners had a competitive advantage over the rest of the world through their advanced education and training, but as I look at the MBA classes I teach at Johns Hopkins University, I see that the majority of my students are from China, Korea, India, and other countries whose economies are growing at near double-digit rates. When I ask these students what they intend to do with their degrees, their answers have changed over the years. It used to be that they wanted to stay in the United States. Now, most aspire to go home to their own country where their professional opportunities are greater. For some time now businesses have learned they can find good, English-speaking, U.S.-trained talent in Shanghai, Seoul, and New Delhi who work for salaries that are less than half of their U.S. counterparts and whose access to the Internet is just as effective as those working from their homes in a U.S. suburb.

This is a "Brave New World" that Huxley never envisioned. But it is clear that as we talk about such issues as we do practically every day, we would do well to realize that there are now literally millions of talented, hard-working, well-trained professionals elsewhere in the world who are happy to do our jobs!

Leading the Way in a Flattened World

Professional Standards and Education Grow in Importance

Two books that go a long way to explaining our world, how we got to where we are, and the factors that will determine where we are going are

Guns, Germs, and Steel (W. W. Norton & Co., 1999) by Jared Diamond and *The World Is Flat* (Farrar Straus & Giroux, 2005) by Thomas Friedman.

Readable and well researched, the two works complement each other: Diamond shows how the forces of geology, climate, and natural resources shaped the way civilizations emerged in history, although Friedman portrays the modern world as it has become through technology, trade, and the dominance of free-market economic principles. Both sketch a world and future where the traditional work of nonprofit organizations—especially standards setting, education, training, and networking—is and will be key.

Big Questions

Diamond focuses on really big questions. For example, why did European civilization become so dominant in the world? How did it happen that Europeans conquered and colonized the Americas and enslaved Africans—why didn't the opposite happen?

Diamond demonstrates how the balance of power over the ages has been determined by the available natural resources, such as a moderate climate, cultivable soil, animals that could be domesticated and used for power and transportation, and a geographic position that lends itself to trade or attack from neighbors. His analysis is presented so clearly and his insight so original that each chapter is an "Aha!" moment for the reader.

Friedman then talks about the dawning of a new age, the one in which we are living now, where the traditional shaping forces described by Diamond have been replaced. According to Friedman, the world has been made "flat" through technology and the lowering of philosophical, legal, and economic barriers to travel, trade, and the exchange of ideas.

With the globe's resources equally available to anyone, anywhere—witness the Chinese purchase of a Canadian oil concern in Latin America, and the success of "virtual" businesses in which global talent as well as goods and services are brought together and exchanged through electronic means—what are the new factors that will determine future balances of power? For Friedman, the new balance of power increasingly resides in the kind and quality of education and training available to any given population group.

In a Flat World

In a "flat" world where there is less and less "friction" in seeking and obtaining the resources to get things done, most of the keys to success can be found in a person's head. Friedman quotes Bill Gates as stating that, in this world, he would prefer to be born a brilliant person in Mumbai than a person of average abilities in New York.

This was not always the case, of course. Until recently a person, through no credit of his own, could thank his lucky stars to be born in a middle-class family in the United States, because with reasonable effort and discipline, this person could expect a comfortable, hassle-free lifestyle. Now the rules of the game have changed. All things being equal, Friedman asks, who has the advantage when the French are trying to figure out how to shorten their workweek though India is trying to fit a workweek into a single day?

In this fluid, flat world, professional standards and professional education and training are king. These factors are what increasingly will distinguish the "haves" from the "have-nots," and savvy students, businesses, and consumers know it.

These are the areas where nonprofits typically dominate—or do they? A number of years ago, the Washington Post Company noted that more than 50 percent of its revenues came not from their news operations, but from their for-profit learning centers around the world that focus on helping students and professionals improve their skills. For-profit companies are entering the education and training arena because demand is booming and so are the profits.

Education and training within the framework of professional standards are defining the new balance of power. The association world needs to determine how best to grasp this opportunity because in this newly flattened world, everything must be earned, and competition often comes from unexpected sources.

The Rise of SMEs in the Global Arena

In the early 1990s an interesting phenomenon was noted by certain national government agencies such as the U.S. Department of Commerce and commented on in international business and policy forums such as the World Economic Forum in Davos, Switzerland. For the first time since records have been kept, the greatest gains in cross-border commercial transactions were being registered by small and medium-size enterprises (SMEs). Although the large multinational companies (MNCs) in the fields of computer technology, aerospace, and agriculture still accounted for the largest share of world trade, anyone could already see that this would not always be the case if the SMEs continued in this jaw-dropping trend.

How did and do these little companies and the new start-ups do it? They do not have the budget to pay for legions of lawyers and international market researchers, nor do they have employees in offices the world over. Basically there are two answers: the Internet, and their use of and membership in trade associations, professional societies, and chambers of commerce that provide them access to professional and product standards that are recognized internationally, market intelligence, and valuable business contacts.

In fact, it could be argued that the Internet and these many kinds of nonprofit business associations were the first to provide SMEs the tools to take advantage of the new market opportunities that were just opening in central and eastern Europe as well as China and other parts of Asia—even though the larger multinational companies were shackled to their bloated payrolls and brick-and-mortar edifices in markets that were offering only flat or declining returns. The Internet and business associations provided SMEs the low-cost infrastructure support they needed to beat the big guys to new markets in a way and on a scale that has never before happened.

But not all associations realized what a gold mine they were sitting on as they continued to focus their attention on the "old dependables." Even as wringing their hands at the challenges globalization was bringing to their memberships, many associations did not fathom the clever ways the "smaller" members were using these same resources to catapult themselves into the global arena.

What was also happening in these same associations was that increasing numbers of foreign nationals were realizing that they offered ways into the domestic market as well. By accessing the standards-making and training and networking programs that these associations offered, nationals from developing countries in regions such as Africa, Asia, and Latin America were taking advantage of quick and easy ways to penetrate the markets of the world's more developed economies. It is no wonder that beginning in the 1990s associations began to see sales of their publications and program attendance for foreign-based customers running at growth trends of more than two to one over their domestic customers. But since the absolute numbers were still relatively low, these trends escaped the attention of most who continued to be preoccupied and worried about the economic changes they were witnessing

Opportunities in the Face of Declining Membership: How to Survive When Dealing with Industry Consolidation

Like the animated cartoon figures that keep on running on thin air over and past a cliff until they suddenly realize there is no longer any ground underneath them, associations often continue functioning in a "business as usual" mode until they realize their traditional membership support is not coming back.

Although it is funny watching the expression on cartoon figures' faces change the instant before they drop like rocks, it is not so funny watching the decline and fall of associations. As an association leader who might be faced with declining membership due to any of a variety of causes—not the least of which might be due to the effects of the Great Recession—what, if anything, can you do to avoid this fate?

First, you should be reassured that your association is far from being alone when it comes to declining membership. This nearly universal decline in membership, for trade associations and professional societies alike, is due to four overriding trends (note that these trends, in and of themselves have potentially negative consequences for traditionally focused nonprofits. At the same time, they offer new, entrepreneurial positive opportunities for nonprofits that are flexible and quick enough to respond):

- Over the past two decades, a globalizing economy has led to increased levels of mergers and acquisitions in virtually every economic sector. Companies are seeking increased efficiencies and are trying to better position themselves to serve and compete in new markets. Global competitiveness, combined with the recent economic downturn, has led many companies to reduce long-term research budgets, focusing instead on short-term applied research that offers immediate market advantages for their products. This concern with short-term competitiveness has also resulted in reduced or eliminated budgets that formerly supported employee association dues, seminars, events and travel.

- Technology is changing at an ever-increasing rate, causing whole industries to disappear. Computer leasing (others include the fabric industry, materials engineering, etc., have all left the United States and relocated to Asia) is one industry that was thriving in the 1960s, 70s, and 80s when computers were huge and expensive. Now that computers are pocket-sized and affordable, this multimillion-dollar subsector of the leasing industry disappeared virtually overnight. However, technology is also creating new industries (such as in health care with magnetic resonance imaging [MRI] and positron emission tomography [PET] scan equipment manufacturers and users).
- As a communications and information access vehicle, the easy-to-use, inexpensive, and instantaneous Internet has made networking, education and training, business transactions, marketing, and the exchange of ideas affordable and available to virtually everyone. Faced with this reality, it is not unusual that the value and relevance of traditional association membership and face-to-face meetings and events should be increasingly called into question.
- A generational aversion to "joining," born of watching the upward and downward ties of loyalty dissolve between employer and employee. Many younger staffers believe that loyalty does not pay and financial security is based on networking and having and maintaining the skills set and credentials needed to be relevant in a rapidly changing economy. Among many in the younger generation there is perceived to be no intrinsic value in joining an association; you buy what you want and move on, even if it means paying a nonmember price for an event, publication, training, or other desired product. This perspective has a direct negative impact on association membership recruiting/retention, but offers a new opportunity for marketing to nonmembers.

These trends have certainly created a changed scenario for the association world, but not a totally bleak one. Despite what is happening to the majority, some associations are actually seeing their membership grow. Some associations have indeed benefited from these trends and increased their membership by pursuing niche strategies. Others seem to have resisted the laws of physics and have grown their programs, publications, and finances despite declines in membership.

The niche approach includes growth through acquisition—picking off competing associations that have fallen on hard times—or by creating a new association to serve the needs of a new growth sector in the economy. This approach is not long-term focused—tactical, not strategic. A strategic perspective is needed if an association is to enjoy any sort of security beyond the next few years.

Managers must realize that although the four long-term trends present undeniable challenges, each also presents "critical opportunities," critical because, to adapt a phrase from *The Godfather*, these are opportunities you can't refuse (although it has been shown time and again that volunteer and staff leaders can and do refuse to see and act on these opportunities, preferring to pursue business as usual, waiting for "things to return to normal"). Seeing and acting on these opportunities requires a keen entrepreneurial mind-set and decision making. It certainly takes more than a one-year perspective and set of values by nonprofit leadership. This one-year vision may be the single biggest obstacle for many nonprofits.):

1. Business consolidation is a reality that will continue for the foreseeable future. Rather than pinning their futures on diminishing membership numbers, associations that are thriving are seeking to make themselves indispensable for what they can do that for-profits cannot.

(Many nonprofits justifiably have a respectable "third-party broker" status derived from their ability to bring many diverse interests to the table for resolution and action on key issues.)

Associations can serve as liaisons between government or the public at large and private-sector interests; compile industry-wide statistics on business, social, human resource, and other economic trends; design and promote professional and manufacturing credentials; and serve as a resource for continuing education and training.

Some associations, seeing declines in their traditional U.S. market, are designing globalization strategies of their own—taking their considerable store of intellectual and financial resources into fast growth markets abroad where sister societies have yet to take root.

2. The pace of technological change will only continue to increase, as will its impact on business and professions. Associations that have adapted best to this have made the change part of their culture. They annually undertake top-to-bottom strategic planning, and identify emerging trends. (This trend helps to create value for nonprofits that are in the standards-setting business by continuing to develop and promulgate global standards needed for new technologies to be implemented around the world. Global standards help facilitate international expansion, trade and commerce, as well as education and learning opportunities for individuals, corporations and emerging nation economies. Opportunities for global standards, however, are not limited to technologies; e.g., SHRM is an example of a nonprofit successfully developing global standards in the human resource field.)
3. The Internet's impact simply cannot be underestimated. Association publications are now available through the Internet. Education and training programs, virtual conferences, and networking through mailing list servers and chat rooms are also important services associations can provide. Online testing and certification services are likely to follow. If your association is not on this train, it should be! (The global Internet has become more than a source for information. It has also become for many persons a source of networking and individual contacts, e.g., Twitter, Facebook, YouTube, etc. This was formerly one of the greatest assets of traditional nonprofits, i.e., the opportunity to network with those of similar interest, career field, etc.)
4. Associations that are growing the fastest are measuring growth by users/consumers of products and services and not members. Rather than trying to fight this trend of declining membership loyalty, successful associations have defined themselves according to the market they serve and taken steps to ensure they serve it well. (How should nonprofits measure growth and success in the future? Is it by traditional membership head counts? Is it by revenue, either dues-based or non-dues-based? How should future success be defined and measured?)

Outwit, Outplay, Outlast: Today's Associations Need Creativity, Imagination, and a New Focus to Survive

Several decades ago, a New York City–based business association conducted a critical analysis of its competitive advantages. The association learned that it had a good, nationwide membership base of business leaders who, as a whole, had a profound impact on the nation's economy.

On the basis of this observation, association staff members developed a periodic survey to find out how these business leaders viewed the economy—were they optimistic or pessimistic? The survey became a benchmark that has a profound impact on the stock markets as well as national fiscal and economic policies. The association's staff members discovered a competitive advantage that they had been sitting on all along, but until then had never imagined its use in this way.

In this era of rapid economic, technical, social, and political change, nonprofits are entering a season where the inefficient and irrelevant are being winnowed out. In this Darwinian selection process, what factors determine which associations survive?

The organizations that are doing best are those that have adopted a market-focused approach in defining their strategies and structuring their operations. But what has this done to the more traditional "member-focused" strategy that has always constituted the core element of association thinking?

Although the "high touch," personal approach is still important—and technology is providing the means to track and serve the individual likes and dislikes of larger groups or people—the evidence shows this isn't enough to resist the tide of diminishing loyalty that's affecting virtually every membership-based organization around the world.

Contrary to this evidence, association leaders are spending fabulous amounts of time and financial resources trying to do just that. Some, in a desperate effort to avoid their fate, stake everything on member-get-a-member, sponsorship, and direct-mailing tactics in attempts to rebuild their membership bases—with results two or three years later that show they indeed had only delayed the inevitable. They have failed to do what Tom Peters calls "reimagining" their organization.

Why is this so pervasive among many nonprofits? Why is this "business as usual" adopted by many volunteers and staff leaders? One of the primary reasons is the "one-year perspective" that results from many volunteer leaders serving only one year in their top leadership role, combined with little or no accountability for organizational results, either during their leadership year or thereafter, as organizational consequences become apparent for business decisions made during their leadership year.

The "one-year vision" is counterproductive to strategic planning (by definition, concerned with periods of time longer than a year) and often results in operational budgets and resources focused largely, if not entirely, on the fiscal year's programs and activities, preventing the nonprofit from becoming an entrepreneurial and innovative activity. Hence, business as usual becomes virtually an automatic annual process. This is a major organizational challenge.

Adapting to the Environment

One method that some association leaders are using to take a new and critical look at their organizations is to imagine what it might mean for them to be truly "market driven" instead of "member focused." This might seem like blasphemy, but bear with me.

The classic "member-focused," relationship-based association defines itself according to the members it serves. A market-focused, performance-based organization defines itself according to its competitive advantages.

The difference is striking. Members of a professional engineering society, for example, have undergone a fact-based reimagining of their organization. Although it is among the largest and most sophisticated engineering societies in the world, it's serving an ever-diminishing pool of U.S. engineers. The pool is shrinking because many of the lower-order engineering jobs are moving offshore, and the core of mechanical engineering has been reimagined by engineers in totally new fields of engineering such as nanotechnology and biotechnology.

Rather than shrinking along with the definition of its historic membership base, the society determined it would be market driven and that it would mobilize its vast skills and resources to serve the field as it has evolved into global markets and new fields of technology.

Such a market-focused approach inserts marketing into a new strategic role—one that for associations could well spell the difference between survival and the alternative. (Such a perspective also enables volunteer and staff leadership to look beyond a "one-year perspective" and to focus vision, energy, and resources over a longer-term, strategic vision that includes global markets and emerging trends, with budgets and resources for entrepreneurial and innovative activities.)

Following Market Drivers to New Destinations

Associations are finding success in adapting business practices from the for-profit sector for their own use, and this includes the discipline of detecting and targeting market trends. One nascent trend is the concept of creating a market-focused organization—an organization that defines itself by being active in detecting and positioning itself to serve new needs in a rapidly changing environment, rather than simply responding to member requests.

Such organizations identify not only market trends but their own competitive opportunities and advantages—those areas in which they are uniquely positioned to address what might be either opportunities or threats.

To a certain extent it makes sense that smaller enterprises are better suited to take advantage of the quickly evolving needs of a global marketplace in a quick and cost-effective way. But, unlike the slower-moving, large, multinational corporations, the smaller entities often do not have either the infrastructure or the resources to easily gather the information needed to do that. For these services, they must rely on outside providers, including government resources, chambers of commerce, and—most importantly—business and professional associations. Market-driven U.S. associations have recognized the advantage of positioning themselves to provide such services to this fast-growing segment of the U.S. economy, including:

- Gathering market statistics
- Researching potential partners
- Finding and training staff
- Informing members of the legislative and regulatory environment in potential markets

In addition, the smart trade associations have either anticipated or followed their members' emerging needs in foreign markets by setting up chapters abroad or establishing strategic alliances with sister organizations.

Roles for Professional Societies / Individual Member Organizations (IMOs)

Professional societies and other IMOs can also position themselves to take advantage of these trends. Many societies have recognized that both U.S. and multinational organizations that employ their members have serious education, training, and quality-evaluation needs as they enter foreign markets. Although these organizations remain single-member societies, they have identified and formed mutual help alliances with their particular market drivers—those organizations (including both corporations and governmental entities) that employ the professionals the societies are intended to serve. Often, it is the employer that pays for the employee association dues and participation expenses, including time away from the job. Thus, many IMOs are beginning to see that employers of the association's individual members are a key market and ally for the IMO. Innovative associations are working closely with employers to tailor and develop value-added programs, services, and marketing for employers, such as education, training, and certification for their U.S. and global workforce.

Turning Challenge into Opportunity

As we read, hear, and see more evidence of the outsourcing of U.S. jobs, the professional societies that serve those segments of the employment picture that are vulnerable to outsourcing have found themselves with fewer and fewer U.S. members, not necessarily because they are doing a poor job of serving their members but because the total pool of potential members in the United States is actually declining. For some organizations, this situation heralds a bleak future. But for others that remain focused on recognizing these trends and identifying the market drivers behind them, the situation can turn into a tremendous opportunity for U.S. and global growth. Therein lies the principal distinction between the winners and losers among nonprofit organization functioning in the global economy.

Putting the Market in the Driver's Seat

For generations the key to successful association management was in taking care of your members. Know their names and apply a lot of tender loving care and the membership numbers will take care of themselves.

However, for the past decade, associations as well as professional societies have found it increasingly difficult to attract and to retain members. In response, association managers have resorted to every membership marketing technique conceivable, including "improved member communications," incentive gifts, discounts, and other special treatment of one kind or another. Yet in most cases the return on investment has been disappointing. How frustrating, then, for these managers to witness associations that seem to attract members effortlessly.

An association of internal auditors represents such a case. Although the managers work hard to be responsive to member needs, the underlying secret to their success is tied to the same causes that have made attracting and retaining members such a nightmare for associations: They have identified, defined, and set themselves up to deliver the cutting-edge products and services needed by an increasingly insecure and competitive market.

In virtually every survey of association membership, the first advantage people cite for belonging to an organization is networking. But networking is really only a fringe benefit of a program or organization that has succeeded in attracting a critical mass of people and companies in the first place. (As previously discussed, the Internet and social media now offer networking opportunities that appeal to many people, and opportunities that are often more convenient, at lower or no cost.) In the general camaraderie of association meetings, it is easy for association managers to lose track of the somewhat stark fact that people are there because they are seeking to acquire the competitive advantages they need to survive. The tools that give them "survivability" consist of enhanced professional skills, knowledge, and experience of best-practice methodologies, and the marketable diplomas or certificates that certify their level of expertise.

This association of internal auditors had studied its market and had developed these tools. In addition, they had effectively established their brand image as the only reputable place where these products and services could be acquired. As a result of this preparation, they have seen double-digit revenue growth—the bulk of which comes through the sale of its products and services to nonmembers at nonmember prices. The association's membership has also grown, but this is a secondary benefit, not the driving factor behind the association's strategy.

Being market driven can open vast new possibilities for associations. In the preceding example, the association realized that its market was global in scope and that in fact the opportunities outside the United States were far greater than in the domestic market alone. Although it is a professional society serving the needs of the individuals in a given profession, the association also discovered a useful niche in serving the professional training needs of corporations and government. Being strictly a traditional member-focused organization (i.e., simply listening to existing members and trying to give them what they say they want) is to be blind to new opportunities. This association demonstrates that a market-driven approach is the way to thrive in a competitive global market.

In this scenario, members are indeed important. Their input guides the organization and the products and services it develops and delivers. But these members are attracted to the organization precisely because it serves a market that is far bigger than the membership itself—and that has been the key to the association's success!

Is a Global Strategy Beyond Your Means?

Affordability is a term that comes up a lot when association executives discuss international programs, members, and issues. In this difficult economy, most association executives find it politically easier within their organizations to focus their intellectual and financial resources entirely on domestic activities (this is where the "one-year vision" syndrome is so pervasive—resulting in business as usual.) But such decisions should not be taken lightly. If care were taken to examine the opportunities that are thus being lost in the international arena, association executives might well see that they are sacrificing their organizations' future relevancy for questions that are far more short term and that have far less strategic value.

If past performance has been any indication, "international" has proven to be a prudent investment choice—as measured by rates of growth. When comparing the growth of imports and exports with the growth of the overall economy in the United States over the past four decades, it is easy to see that the international segment of the country's economy, cross-cutting nearly every sector, has consistently grown twice to three times faster than the domestic side. Most U.S. associations can see this pattern mirrored in their own growth figures.

But there is much more at stake internationally for associations right now than even strong growth potential. There are three current windows of opportunity where international infrastructures are being created that are going to have a determining influence in deciding which associations are going to be the world's most relevant players 10 years from now—and these are the organizations companies and professionals are going to want to join.

Before deciding to cut back or eliminate funding for "international" programs, association executives would do well to measure how effectively they are positioned to take advantage of these three global trends that are shaping their and their members' futures:

1. *A growing need to share ideas and information on a global basis.* This need is in direct response to both threats and opportunities.

   As an example of a threat, contrast the unchecked worldwide spread of the Spanish influenza epidemic of 1917–1918 that claimed more lives than were lost during all of World War I, to the rapid global response and coordination of governments and health care authorities in 2003 that resulted in the far more limited toll of the deadly severe acute respiratory syndrome (SARS) virus. How much more deadly would SARS have been if we did not have these global health care research and governance structures, the Internet, and easy and rapid international travel—all tools and drivers of our global economy—to combat it? All organizations—whether in health care, law enforcement, or other—are seeking to create the global communications networking, research, and information exchange programs that are needed to combat global threats—be they from viruses or terrorists.

As an example of an opportunity, associations should compare and contrast the growth trends of U.S. versus non-U.S. programs and membership in their own and rival associations. Those organizations that do so find without exception that non-U.S. growth rates are inevitably greater (most times by factors of two or three) than domestic U.S. trends. The reasons behind this are simple enough. For the past six decades the average per capita incomes and education levels of the world's population have steadily increased. This has naturally led to an increased demand for the best and most affordable products and services the world over; and in a six billion–person world, these demands can be very powerful indeed.

2. *A growing need to define common standards.* With the almost exponential growth of world trade has come the need for common industry and professional standards. The Geneva-based International Standards Organization (ISO) has claimed this role—but, to date, U.S. commercial participation in this effort has been generally much less than what has come from Europe. As a result, ISO-developed and -promoted standards are likely to prove much more advantageous to most Europeans than to the United States on the global economic competitive field. Hence, development of globally accepted standards by and with U.S. participation is an opportunity and an advantage. Many associations are well positioned for standards development with global participation.
3. *A growing need for capacity building in the developing world's economies.* The developing world does not just want to be consumers of the developed world's products; they aspire to be part of the developed world themselves. In this regard, there is a huge and growing need for transferring knowledge and learning to the developing world's economies in what international development economists call capacity building. Recently, there has been a renewed emphasis in funding international education and training programs through the World Bank, the United Nations, and the U.S. Agency for International Development—programs in

which most U.S. associations historically do not participate. As with standards development, many U.S. associations are well known for education, training, and certification programs, in addition to standards development, making those associations leaders in capacity building and all that goes with it.

Each of the three trends just noted is shaping the world in very definitive ways. Those associations and professional societies and their members that are participants in this process will find it much easier to operate in the world 10 years from now than those that are not. Viewed in this light, it seems shortsighted indeed for any association to assert that it cannot afford to participate. Does the old English saying describing how "for want of a nail a war was lost" apply in this case to some in the association community?

Once association executives and their members appreciate the relevancy of what is at stake, perhaps affordability becomes less of an issue. But are the costs of being a player in these arenas really that prohibitive? Providing a forum or network for exchanging ideas, developing standards, and providing training and education—these are areas that represent the bulk of what most associations and professional societies do; all that is missing is to provide the international linkage. Even when means are limited, there are at least three cost-effective ways of doing this:

1. Forming strategic alliances with sister organizations around the globe in which common goals are identified and complementary services rendered. (Working together with global allies and partners not only makes entry into and activities in a country more successful, but the information and service exchange enhances all the partners and participants. Almost no nonprofit should expect to simply "export" their programs and services to another country and be well received by the host country, sister organizations, and individuals.)
2. Expanding use of the Internet to incorporate international input and to provide products and services that have international appeal electronically.
3. Positioning your organization to participate in the vastly expanding government-funded programs that are designed to assist developing markets around the world.

None of these tactics are particularly expensive to implement. But if any further incentive is needed, picture what your association's members will do 5 or 10 years from now when they look at the associations from which they have to choose. Is your association among those that are: defining world standards; providing global networking, research, and communications opportunities; and developing special links with new emerging markets around the world? If it is, then you can congratulate yourself on your stewardship. If it is not, then will you be able to console yourself that at least you saved some money this year?

Associations Could Profit from Global Opportunities

One of the many lessons learned as a consequence of September 11, 2001, is that no one in the developed world can afford to overlook the plight of the impoverished countries whose struggling economies and weak governments provide a natural breeding ground for extremists.

The U.S. government, along with governments of developed countries around the world, have pledged record levels of financial support for education and training programs designed to give the world's poorest countries the know-how to build and maintain agricultural, financial, health, political, and social infrastructures.

All of these programs are run through organizations such as the World Bank, the United Nations, the regional development banks, and bilateral development agencies such as the U.S. Agency for International Development.

For the most part, these development agencies do not run these programs themselves, they bid them to specialists in the private sector. These specialists traditionally have come from the many consulting firms that have sprung up in the Washington, D.C., area for the sole purpose of winning such project assignments.

With additional funds and more complex needs, the World Bank, the U.S. Agency for International Development (USAID), and the UN are seeking to expand the range of talent available to them, and are looking to nonprofits. The rationale is that nonprofits have their hearts in the right place, and they have proved to be more adept than consulting

SETH,

This book is currently being read/used by the Board of Directors in our efforts to "Go Global" & have all CEDIA offices operate as one. This book was also written by our consultant - Steve Worth who will be giving a presentation at the February Board meeting. Please read/familarize yourself with this prior to our meeting next week.

Ashley

CEDIA®

CUSTOM
ELECTRONIC
DESIGN &
INSTALLATION
ASSOCIATION

firms in replicating themselves—leaving behind self-sustaining trade and business associations that continue the work that was started.

U.S. associations have an unprecedented opportunity to do well by doing good, particularly those in high-demand sectors, such as agriculture, health care, construction, and engineering, and disciplines that provide the skills to properly build and manage a business.

Many U.S. association executives are assessing the challenges and opportunities of the global marketplace, but are finding it hard to convince members to invest the association funds needed to start an international membership program. In this regard, government-funded international education and training programs are a golden opportunity to travel abroad, lend a hand, and help appreciative people. Doing so also creates contacts that can and do translate into new international friends and members for the association

It pays for association executives to take the time to investigate these programs. One Florida-based professional society has been particularly skillful in bidding on and winning contracts from the World Bank and USAID. The association produces training materials used mostly by retired members who appreciate the opportunity to travel to exotic lands, transfer skills, and make a difference in the lives of the people they meet.

The association also benefits from a financially profitable activity. It provides associations yet another arrow in the quiver of membership services. And it has slowly allowed associations to build a global network of members and strategic contacts that could evolve into overseas chapters.

This is a win-win situation all around. For the U.S. government agencies that sponsor these programs, it is an opportunity to show the best of the United States and its people. And for U.S. associations, this is an opportunity to "go global" in a way that is very relevant to their members—and to make some money while they are at it!

Assisting Countries in Need with Associations' Missions

Billions of dollars are spent each year to help develop the economic infrastructures of developing and new market economies around the world.

These moneys are channeled through programs administered by USAID, the World Bank, Inter-American Development Bank, Asian Development Bank, African Development Bank, and European Bank for Reconstruction and Development, just to name a few. There are also organizations funded by the European Union (EU) and its member states; the governments of Canada, Australia, and Japan; as well as numerous private foundations, like the Soros Foundation, that administer service in many of the same markets.

These agencies represent the source of funding; however, the actual service work is performed by other organizations. Some of the work is handled by nongovernmental organizations such as Catholic Charities, but most are handled by the larger consulting as well as those consulting operations specializing in international development, such as Chemonics International, Development Alternatives International, ABT Associates, Management Systems International, and others.

Five years ago, USAID published the white paper *New Partnerships Initiative: A Strategic Approach to Development Partnering*, announcing their intent to involve more nonprofits in their development work. The agency's reasoning for this new focus on the association community stems from the purposes around which these organizations are created.

Associations exist to serve those in need and primarily emphasize nonfinancial returns. As a result, participation in cause-related programming generally falls within their missions. In short, the association community's missions complement USAID's program objectives. More important, USAID believes that involving associations is key to the sustainability of its programs around the world.

In order to establish the close relationships and long-term programming, USAID now more than ever is seeking program managers who will remain committed long after contract funding has been exhausted. Collaborating with the association community holds this hope of longevity that has become a priority for USAID.

To date, few associations have taken advantage of the opportunities available through a USAID partnership initiative and other such programs.

One reason for the limited participation by associations has to do with the labor-intensive and highly complicated nature of bidding for and managing foreign programs. Associations generally do not have the expertise on staff to navigate through the process. In addition, associations have been reluctant to make the necessary resource investment without first obtaining some assurance of a return.

Associations and their consultants can work together to bridge this gap and develop the administrative tools and funding required to launch or broaden their work in international markets through these government-funded programs.

Those associations that decide to participate will likely find the results incredibly satisfying and rewarding.

Making the Case to Go Global

Polls taken in the United States since September 11, 2001, indicate that more than a majority of Americans see the need for and the importance of globalization. The most interesting thing about these polls is how dramatically this percentage goes up within audience groups characterized as "managers" or "senior executives." Within these "leadership" groups the response is typically above 90 percent for those who see globalization as an important trend for the United States and its economy. Association executives should fall within these elite groups, but it is mystifying how many of these senior executives, who have front row seats to the impact of globalization, remain as mute and inexpressive as tree stumps during board meetings when globalization is discussed.

These executives likely know that association boards are fickle things and it is better to be accommodating than the standing nail that invites hammering! Indeed, the cautious manager sees that association boards are often inclined to be skeptical about the benefits of globalization. Boards by nature and by responsibility tend to be locally focused because a principal part of their responsibility is to ensure the association is serving its members and shareholders and resources are being used by and for them.

This begs the question: is there anything executives can do to frame the debate so boards can see better how and why globalization is important to their associations' members? One way is to quantify the impact globalization is having in strategic areas of interest for the association's members. But this effort is time consuming and ultimately effective only if your audience is already open-minded enough to listen.

After reviewing the numbers in this way, one CEO of a major U.S. association (over 70 percent of whose members are based in the United States) stepped aside and invited his executive team to list what they saw as the pros and cons of going global. The group seemed to be fairly evenly divided between those who could see the benefits of going global and those who were opposed.

Among cons, they listed operational and strategic problems of decentralization and risk of dilution of their core message and values. They also listed their fear that the organization would become politicized and be reduced to responding to political forces rather than member needs. Finally, they listed their concern that cultural differences would lead to professional differences.

Among the pros listed were global acceptance of products; larger knowledge and networking base; greater prestige; and, perhaps most tellingly, to have a greater global influence on credentials and standards.

Having compared the lists, the association decided their future was in going global. Leaders did not dismiss the impact the cons were going to have on their efforts, but even taking these into account, they decided they could not afford to have their association stand on the sidelines and let globalization pass them by. They then proceeded to construct a five-year plan to go global.

Association executives cannot fall asleep at the helm, content that global currents will sweep their association along with them. These currents are not always friendly and do heap victims onto the shoals. This happens most often to associations whose leaders have not carefully planned their course.

In his recent book, *The Paradox of American Power* (Oxford University Press, 2002), Joseph S. Nye addresses the difficult question posed by the United States' sheer size and wealth. If you are so much bigger than everyone else, why not go it alone? Why go through the pain and suffering of trying to achieve collaboration and consensus when one is self-sufficient in nearly all things?

Association executives should know the answer better than anyone. Consensus building is the lifeblood of associations, and successful executives know that without it they cannot survive. Nye makes the case that the same is true for our entire country. What is the secret to making a successful case for global expansion? Awareness of the facts is important, but it starts with leadership. Like it or not, if association managers are among those that are the most aware of the importance and impact of globalization, it is their responsibility to prepare their organizations for it.

Rising to the Challenge

The globalizing world we live in is reeling from problems that the traditional economic and political order seem ill-equipped to handle with its antiquated machinery of governance. It is, in fact, a situation tailor-made to those organizations dedicated to the public good, but can they rise to the challenge?

The Primary Challenge

How will historians characterize our times? After the fall of the Soviet Union, Francis Fukuyama famously declared the "end of history." With Western liberal democracy the definitive "winner," nothing more need be said or written!

But it doesn't feel like we are winners, does it? For the first time in our country's history we are facing the very real possibility that a succeeding generation will live less well than the preceding one. We are definitely not entering the land of milk and honey; it is more like the land of rising temperatures, pollution, and competition for scarce resources on a global scale. Rather than an ideological struggle, our times will be marked by how we handle what sociologists call the "tragedy of the commons"—a struggle that nonprofit organizations are uniquely qualified to address.

The tragedy of the commons is a social phenomenon characteristic of human activity throughout the world. Its thesis is that individuals take care of what personally belongs to them, but they tend to abuse and rush to exploit resources that are shared in common, in their haste to get what they can for themselves before these resources run out entirely.

This human tendency to see no further than our own limited interest has always existed, of course, but, apart from a few sociologists and environmentalists, it did not attract a great deal of attention until relatively recently. Now, with global warming reaching a tipping point, global fisheries in full collapse, and every other shared global resource in crisis, even ordinary citizens are starting to realize the impact six billion human souls are having on our planet. Something has to give.

It seems a natural fit that nonprofit organizations could/should be especially involved in all of the critical issues stemming from these "tragedies of the commons." Nonprofit organizations are by definition enterprises that are intended to benefit society; to this point, they are or should be the antithesis of the tragedy of the commons.

Can human behavior be changed in a democratic society that respects individual rights and free enterprise? There is ample evidence that it can, but in this, historically governments and corporate communities both have ambitions and competencies that are regarded with a certain amount of skepticism by the general public—and perhaps rightfully so. An overly aggressive government—be it local, national, or multinational—is sometimes seen as a menace to individual liberties, although unfettered corporations are often seen as rapacious. Only the nonprofit community has the vocation, public trust, and competency to fill this role as a catalyst for societal change. Or does it?

The Secondary Challenge

The time may be right for the nonprofit community to play a historic role in our society and in the global community at large, but will these organizations be up to the challenge? Traditionally, there are three categories of key strategic and organizational issues that challenge the effectiveness of nonprofits. These relate to relevancy, insightfulness, and efficiency/effectiveness. As volunteer leaders, here are the kinds of questions you should be asking your organization:

Are you responding to market need?

- If you are a membership organization, are your members representative of the market as a whole?
- How have you segmented your markets and do your products and services match the needs of each?

- Are your products and services perceived to set the market standard?
- Are your sales figures matching or exceeding market growth rates year to year, and do your prices more than cover your costs?

Are you preparing for where these needs will have moved in 5, 10, or 15 years?

- What percentage of your annual resources—as measured in terms of time and money—are spent in new product development, market surveys, benchmarking, and trend analysis? At least once every few years, it pays to do some trend analysis and from there to envision what your world will look like in 5, 10, or 15 years. The results can sometimes be heart stopping, or, alternatively, they can produce "eureka" insights. Of course, predictions can sometimes be wrong, but it is also true that "surprising" organizational collapses in retrospect generally tend to be not all that surprising.
- Nonprofit organizations tend to be inward or outward looking—how outward looking is yours? Do you rely on affiliates and/or partnerships, or are you more comfortable in employee and vendor relationships? Do you have high turnover in your volunteer leadership positions—are your leadership positions eagerly sought out by newcomers—or do you typically keep the same volunteer leaders for 6 or 10 years or longer? Do you have any board members from outside your industry to provide an outsider's perspective? If you are seeking to change the world—or at least that part of it that relates to your mission—you need, by definition, to be outwardly focused; and for each and every organization, this requires a conscious effort to achieve.

Are you operating efficiently?

- Are you operating as fast, as efficiently, and as effectively as possible?
- Do you have a clear and recognized brand image/reputation that matches your vision?
- Do you have a memorable and meaningful purpose as perceived by your stakeholders inside and outside your organization?

- Do you have the market-focused tools and resources you need to achieve your mission?

Your challenge in working with volunteer leaders:

- How can you expect to change the world if you cannot attract and constantly replenish your supply of volunteer talent?
- Volunteering implies three things: a voluntary commitment in which all parties (meaning the nonprofit organization itself as well as the volunteers) bring something to the table that the others cannot as easily do for themselves; that each party's strategic goals and missions complement the other's; and that the overriding goal of this voluntary partnership serves a greater purpose. In these respects, volunteering is a partnership.

Ideally, partnerships carry with them at least five benefits:

1. They allow and encourage a sharing of resources—they permit all partners to do more than they could on their own.
2. They allow all to expand their networks of professional contacts.
3. Nonprofit partnerships (ideally) provide an opportunity to do well by doing good.
4. They are enriching experiences through which all parties can learn from each other new ways of doing things.
5. Partnerships allow all concerned to gain greater credibility and influence.

Work is hard—even volunteer work, so it may seem counterintuitive to say that having fun is a good litmus test for the effectiveness of your operations. The ancient Greeks defined happiness as the full employment of one's abilities in endeavors that matter. As serious as the issues are that you and/or your volunteer leaders may be tackling, the work itself should be fun, because you are employing your unique abilities in furtherance of something that matters!

Chapter 2

Common Problems in the Global Arena

Organizations face problems in the global arena. Some problems make the organization stronger and some result in disaster—but in all there is a lesson to be learned on the do's and don'ts of going global. This chapter presents cases that display the real-life problems faced by organizations in the global arena. It concludes with a discussion of what a global problem is and what a local problem is—key concepts, when globalization's success is in how well global concepts are applied to local needs.

Globalization in the New Millennium

Many organizations claim to be international, but if a global organization means that one can operate as easily in any given part of the world as another — then very few organizations are truly global.

"Everybody talks about the weather," Benjamin Franklin once pointed out, "but no one does anything about it." Could the same be true for globalization? How many managers can say their organizations are ready to face the challenges of this global era? Wait! Before you put your hands up, take a look at the globalization efforts of four very different organizations. Do some of their problems and challenges sound familiar?

Case Study 1: An Association of Professional Services Firms

Founded in the early 1980s, a New Jersey–based trade association represents professional service firms in the booming outplacement industry. With growing international membership and concern for the impact of legislation and regulations on its industry, the association relocated to Washington, D.C., where it could better serve the interests of its international members and handle government relations for its U.S. members.

In the decade since its creation, Europe had become the single fastest growth market in the world for outplacement firms and services. By the mid-1990s, North America was considered mature, with slow to flat growth prospects. For this reason, the association's board agreed to restructure "to give greater voice to Europeans and to evolve from being an American-dominated, international association to one that was more global in outlook and governance structure," said Frank Louchheim, founding chairman of Right Management Consulting and current member of the board of the association.

The association encountered three challenges in the restructuring:

1. *Standards.* Small, nationally based outplacement trade associations in Europe had nearly abandoned their efforts to develop professional standards for lack of consensus. Nevertheless, they resisted any attempt by the American association to offer assistance.
2. *Dues.* European dues were not charged the same rate as Americans were charged. When Americans challenged that European members were not paying enough, the Europeans countered their argument by illustrating their many more diverse obligations at the national, regional, and world levels. If all their expenditures were

taken into account, they argued, it would be obvious that the Europeans were, in fact, paying more.

3. *Cost.* The third challenge was to identify the added value of a new, global organization. If there were increased costs associated with creating such an organization, who would pay?

Despite this resistance, the association was able to obtain acceptance of its professional standards and even to reach agreement on a uniform international dues rate. Dues would be paid to the regional chapters, with a small portion allocated to the oversight of its international operations.

The operations of the European organizations were then merged into the newly federated structure of the organization, which was based on geographic regions. Since North America was slightly larger than Europe, it was agreed that the international operations would continue to be based in Washington, D.C.

The next step was to rewrite the association's bylaws to redefine the governance structure of North American, European, and other international affiliates. With membership almost evenly split between Europe and the United States, the worldwide presidency would alternate location between North America and Europe. The worldwide board of directors would give equal representation to North American and European representatives and further provide proportionate representation for every region of the world.

The next challenge was to identify the added value of international or global services for its members, of which there appeared to be few. Since the current newsletter was in English and addressed to our American audience, the Europeans decided to create their own. The only remaining international service was the annual conference, which should have been self-supporting. Another important association service was government relations, but because this service was rendered on a national basis, there was very little that the international organization could contribute. Very little filtered up from the nations and regions that was relevant to the global body.

Although the organization was still heavily focused on the national and regional levels, this new structure offered an opportunity for each component part to compare and contrast what was happening within their home markets to what was happening globally. As slight an advantage as this might seem, it was perceived by their members and potential members to be an attractive asset. Smaller companies saw that they were not immune to international trends. They also were attracted to the idea of being in and among an organization that included large multinational companies that could offer them good partnership or merger opportunities. For the larger companies that already had an international perspective, this global organization was essential. It offered them a way to ensure that their various national offices were plugged into the same worldwide network. It established a framework for devising global standards as and when that inevitable day comes. And it offered a cost-effective way of picking up global market intelligence as well as partners among the smaller national market niche players that also belonged.

There are at least five lessons to note from this experience.

First, although this industry was clearly rooted in the issues and regulations of national markets, the members and prospective members of this association were ultimately more attracted to an organization that offered access to global standards and networking structures. Whenever business operations and interests span the globe—as they do in almost every case—standards-making bodies need to follow suit or risk being displaced by others that do offer more global perspectives. Let's say this is an axiom in the standards-setting world and that when given a choice between an organization that opens the door to global economic opportunities or remaining confined to a local or national market, the global option will win every time.

Second, even though it can be argued (as the Europeans did very compellingly in this case) that a given industry is not ready for a global organization, the real deciding factor is in whether your members feel they are ready. Associations have a hard time forcing a market open that is not ready, and may never be ready, to be opened. But when the "early adapters" in a market begin to show signs that they are ready (in this case, for a more global organization), then associations need to move quickly to fulfill the need or they risk losing ground to the organization that does. The early adapters need to constitute enough of a critical mass to make things happen—but then what do you do with the remaining "slower" adapters? In this case, the more parochial member companies were given a way to collaborate that was inclusive of their interests . . . and then, when they first proved to be recalcitrant, they were given an ultimatum—collaborate or else a parallel organization would be set up as a rival. Sometimes hardball negotiating tactics pay off. It is said that you should never go to the negotiating table unless you are prepared to walk away. In this case, the early adapters did walk away and the slower adapters found they couldn't.

Third, as noted above, when it comes to plans that require the cooperation of others, it is always advisable to have fallback plans. As compelling an argument as you may be able to make, it is impossible to force people to act in the way you might want them to. Even before starting to negotiate, work through the different scenarios ahead of time and know what you are going to do in each. In this case, the early adapters were somewhat surprised by the initial reaction of the Europeans, but they were prepared. They responded coolly and matter-of-factly in a way that brilliantly communicated that this was no bluff—it had been thought through.

Fourth, despite the focus on globalization, never forget that globalization has significance only in a local context. People and organizations exist on a local basis. This is where they have their roots—so any call to globalization needs to be translated into local practice. What will be the practical impact of your approach on a local level? How will things work? How will tapping into global trends benefit your smallest, more locally centered members? If you do not have answers to these questions, you cannot succeed.

Fifth, remember always that money matters. The costs associated with these ideas must be paid. The solution cannot be through a levy of taxes—and in the association community, "taxes" means dues. So if money needs to be found and dues cannot be the solution, then you must identify sources of income related to the sale of products and services. This approach has the dual advantage of calculating which infrastructure costs can be built into your plans as well as justifying the practical utility of your strategy. In this case, the association had a limited number of products and services to offer, so it needed to adopt an organizational structure that offered the advantages of a global approach without great additional cost.

Case Study 2: A Large International Accounting Firm

In 1989, the senior partners of two very large international accounting firms negotiated the terms of a merger. The one firm's strong presence in the United States and the other firm's relatively strong presence outside North America created a natural synergy between them both. The two firms would move from seventh and eighth place in the lineup of the "Big Eight" accounting firms, to the third largest place after they merged into one new firm.

Heading Off Disaster. By early 1990, the merger plan faced a pending disaster. The merger had been negotiated by the two firms' largest partnerships in New York City, apparently without fully recognizing the interests of their international partners. However, within one month of the announcement of the New York firms' decision to merge, the one firm's partners in the United Kingdom, Belgium, the Netherlands, and Luxembourg voted down the merger, as did the second firm's partners in Australia and New Zealand. Because these defections were clearly seen as the beginning of a more serious trend of opposition to the merger, damage control would be needed.

If the senior partners of the two firms wanted a global practice, they would need to create a governance structure that gave partners outside of North America a significant role. Since the whole rationale behind the merger in the first place was to create a global practice, there was really no alternative.

Because the U.S. practices (headquartered in New York City) were by far the largest, the most appropriate location for an international headquarters, to be led by an American, was New York. For this structure to gain credibility, however, the management and staff teams running the global firm had to be "international."

The merged firm was given an international name. Partner representatives from all regions comprised the board of directors. And the professional staff consisted of young, English-speaking professionals from both practices in Europe, Latin America, Asia, and Africa. Decisions were made by consensus, and while the opinion of the U.S. partner was dominant, it was also not conspicuous. The U.S. representative took care not to intervene in the day-to-day decision making of the global firm unless he was directly asked or if a critical interest was at stake.

A New Purpose. The immediate mission of the international management team was to develop a unifying vision and mission for the new global firm and to identify the products and services that made this new entity greater than the sum of its parts. Along with this considerable task was the unstated objective of preventing any more defections.

Identifying the products and services of the new, merged firm was difficult. Each firm, with its own products and services, was reluctant to concede superiority. Though progress was slow, creation of an international lending agency (ILA) practice helped. The new firm's ILA practice gave the global firm products and services that were its first tangible benefits of the merger. After some initial capital and personnel investment, the ILA practice became self-supporting.

Overcoming Barriers. The firm's international staff helped assuage the language and cultural differences that existed throughout the worldwide firm, which had grown to encompass 110 countries. Though the working language of the international firm was English, translation and interpretation services were provided and paid for at the national level.

The budget of the international governance structure came from regional contributions, based on a percentage of revenue. Most of the budget was spent on staff travel and paying for the travel of the partners participating in board meetings or in the many committees set up to develop common products, services, and practice standards.

The Dust Settles. By the end of 1993, more than three years after the merger, much of the international staff was disbanded and their budget cut back. The international products and services that had been developed were now delivered on a regional basis. The regional chairs were responsible for the growth of the firm in their respective regions. While products and services were developed and delivered globally through the oversight of international committees, the financial and decision-making power of the firm resided in the regional structures.

The firm might have proceeded much like the association in the first example except that, unlike it, the firm had tough market competition. Since undergoing its first global restructuring, the partnership has restructured itself still further in an effort to create a seamless global organization and is now more closely in line with its toughest competition.

In this example, there are at least two lessons that merit reflection.

First, as large as your key stakeholders may be, no one is large enough to make a far-ranging decision, such as the decision to merge firms, in a vacuum. All your stakeholders must be involved—this is particularly true in an international organization where the larger decision makers may all be of the same nationality. If this happens, national pride almost mandates a certain amount of foot dragging, if not open rebellion, at what surely will be perceived as strong-arm tactics by people with money. Each of us knows what it feels like to be snubbed and overlooked by people who consider themselves more important than we are. This is simple human nature, but when you introduce issues of national and maybe cultural or ethnic pride into the equation, you immediately create a volatile and potentially destructive situation. In this case, the firm did correct itself—albeit a little late. But what would have been better is if they had made this decision a more deliberative process by bringing other nationalities into the picture sooner and soliciting their opinions. There is not as much risk in doing this as might be feared. Time and again focus groups based on nationality conducted by international organizations inevitably come to the same conclusions when presented with the same objective market research results. Their deliberative processes may differ, but they almost always come to the same or very similar conclusions—regardless of their nationality. The end result of such a process is always better, more comprehensive, more thoughtful, and certainly more consensus building. It is the only way to make major decisions in an international environment.

As big and important as the decision makers may be within the organization, their decisions can "die of a thousand cuts" if the decision-making process they follow is not transparent and inclusive of all stakeholders—even the smallest. Arguably, the larger the organization, the more transparency and fact-based decision making is important. Knowing precisely how and why decisions are made is critical to their legitimacy and ultimate acceptance by the rank and file.

More specifically, stakeholders need to be consulted and they need to be able to see that their opinion is reflected in some way in the final decision—even if they do not dominate. Taking these steps is really not all that difficult—and it is far easier to do prior to making a decision than to try to repair damage after the fact, as is the case in this example.

Second, as can be seen in the subsequent development of the international firm into one that is more global in scope and structure, "international" is a dynamic process and not a static end state. Global organizations often start out as nationally focused with an international team driving its finite international transactions. Then, as these international transactions proliferate, the organization becomes more international throughout each of its component parts—thus leading eventually to the time when it no longer needs an international group to drive the process. In effect, the international team has served as a midwife to aid in giving birth to a new organization. But an organization is still international (as opposed to global) if its focus and decision-making structures are still primarily at the national level. Organizations become global when these structures are no longer primarily dependent on national considerations but rather on the shifting demands of global market considerations.

Case Study 3: An International Medical Society

What are the reason(s) for this society's disappointing performance?

This example proves that a global governance structure by itself does not guarantee success in the global marketplace. Founded in 1968, the society represents medical doctors, teachers, and researchers who specialize in the study and treatment of diseases of the skeleton. With more than 700 members worldwide, it holds international conferences (in English) and sponsors the publication of a medical journal (in English, though it is published out of the Netherlands).

Despite strong global growth in all aspects of skeletal research; a long history as an organization; a strong professional journal; strong finances; and a workable, global governance structure, the organization was dying. For a number of years, its membership growth had been stagnant. As members and board members saw new and dynamic organizations growing, they voiced increasing complaints about the lack of direction and purpose at the society. They began openly to question whether their huge savings should not just be given to another organization that could make better use of it. The society president at that time, Dr. Francis Glorieux, recognized that "the time had come to conduct a complete reevaluation of the society and its goals."

The society's board of directors is proportionally chosen according to the society's worldwide membership, which is mostly split between Europe and North America. If there is a regional bias in the organization, it is to non-Americans, since there is great concern that the overwhelming size of the United States could destroy the global character the society seeks to have. Like the association in the first example, the society presidency alternates between North America and Europe. The board has a rotating membership, with nominees presented to the worldwide membership for approval at each annual meeting.

International committees report to the board and oversee the development of member products and services, but do not have adequate time to make these committees function properly. Attendance is also a problem, since volunteers are expected to donate both their time and travel costs.

During a two-day discussion of the critical internal and external factors affecting the society now and in the future, the board concluded that there was indeed a market niche for their association, in spite of the inroads made by other organizations. They reaffirmed their mission and the usefulness of their goals, and developed a list of strategic objectives to be incorporated into an ambitious three-year business plan. As Dr. Glorieux stated, "The single most important action of the board was its recognition that the organization could no longer be run by volunteers alone and its decision that a full-time professional staff was needed."

Indeed, this appears to have made all the difference. Within six months of putting in place a permanent staffing structure, membership had increased by 10 percent. By year's end it had increased by 30 percent.

The key take-away lesson from this case is that strategic direction—even if it is right—is not enough. There also needs to be a way to actually implement and follow through on decisions. The most brilliant strategy needs arms and legs to make it operational—lacking such operational means guarantees failure just as much as having a faulty strategy. In this case, adding an operational component did not involve a great expense and the result was immediate.

International Medical Society for Sale—Anyone? The jury is still out as to whether this organization will succeed, although it looks increasingly unlikely. It has been a year now since it first made the attempt to become global. Nevertheless, there are lessons to be learned from its example.

The organization was conceived as a global association that would unify a wide variety of similarly focused national associations worldwide to develop a more global approach to disseminating and coordinating information on the treatment and prevention of osteoporosis. This strategic move was also supported by the World Health Organization (WHO) in Geneva and a number of large pharmaceutical companies.

"There was every incentive to succeed," says Dr. Larry Raisz, who led the effort. "The support of the WHO and the pharmaceutical companies assured there would be large sums of money to share amongst all players at the end of the effort. And, to a very real extent, the increased information sharing that would result from the creation of such an organization might well lead to the cure or prevention of this growing disease."

The bylaws that were developed are, in many ways, a model for a global association. The proportionate voting governance structure was particularly important. While China and India would have the largest number of members, Europe and the United States would be contributing the largest amount of financial support—without which the organization could not function. These bylaws went through three drafts before final agreement by all participants.

So why has the organization not succeeded in its global launch? Ultimately, it has been a casualty of the tug of war between the Europeans and the North Americans. Seeing the financial incentive all too clearly, the European and American leaders decided that neither wanted to lose control of the organization. To win the financial prizes at stake, North America and Europe were left to divide up the rest of the world.

To date, there is still no global organization unifying the mosaic of associations that currently exists. This organization stands as living proof that where there is no will, there can be no way.

The critical flaws in this example were at least threefold. There was no transparency in the decision-making process—the key stakeholders did not trust each other enough to share their thoughts and concerns openly. They clearly did not have any coherence in what they sought as the purpose of such an organization. And there was little to no consideration given to the actual market needs that this organization would serve. These needs were simply assumed in a vague way as the would-be stakeholders concentrated instead on counting the money that they would never have.

Unfortunately, such examples of misfires are rather commonplace as starry-eyed prospectors rush to mine the gold they hear can be found in globalization, only to find that global streets are not paved with gold. Gold can be made—indeed, it is hard to make it without factoring in the impact of globalization—but it requires preparation and thoughtful hard work.

Cross-Border Collaboration: Sell Successfully Overseas by Learning the Local Needs

Too many U.S. organizations see foreign markets as good "resell" markets—places where they can make an easy profit by reselling U.S. products they've already developed. It is a mistake that even the most sophisticated organizations make.

In 2003, national newspapers in the United States headlined stories (see Neal Gabler's January 9, 2003, article in the *New York Times*, "The World Still Watches America") about overseas television stations that no longer carry American programs on prime time; even the most popular U.S. shows were being relegated to early morning time slots in Asian and European markets. Overseas television programmers, it seems, now prefer to show locally produced shows that they feel are more relevant to local audiences. U.S. association executives, meanwhile, have often seen their books and programs rejected by their sister organizations abroad.

All organizations—associations and others—are under great pressure to sell what is on the shelf. This is sometimes done for reasons that border on cultural chauvinism—the assumption that "We are the best, so why shouldn't everyone buy what we have to offer?"

Americans are known for their marketing savvy; however, when it comes to selling internationally, they tend to ignore the primary marketing rule that they follow religiously at home: know your customers, and give them what they want. The time when Americans could treat overseas markets as dumping grounds for excess or outdated products has reached a close. Americans do not want hand-me-downs, so why should they expect anyone else in the world to accept hand-me-downs?

The curious thing about globalization is that rather than imposing uniformity on the world, it allows individual differences to assert themselves. More nations exist now than at any time since the 18th century, arguably because globalization has empowered people to assert their individuality.

In this climate, the challenge for international marketers is to identify this individuality in any given place. Because associations, more than any other type of organization, depend on consensus building and sensitivity to market trends, they are positioned to take a lead in this area. Global localization is more than a slogan; it is the key to success for international marketing. Identifying market needs is about working with people within the given market to discover those needs.

A Failed Approach

The unsuccessful international initiatives of one association illustrate the importance of customizing products and services for overseas markets. The association, a professional society in the field of health care, was under a great deal of pressure from its board of directors to find additional sources of revenue, and the overseas marketplace seemed rife with possibilities. Having maintained distant contact with their sister organizations around the world, the association's leaders were aware that their organization was larger, better financed, and more sophisticated than any of them. Surely, these overseas organizations would serve as ready markets for the association's many publications, products, and services. The only questions were which ones to sell, in what quantities, and for how much? Or so the association's management thought.

The association hired a market survey expert to poll these potential customers to find out the answers to its questions. After extensive surveying, the consultant reported discouraging results. A number of those surveyed were offended by what they saw as American effrontery—and they said so in no uncertain terms. In fact, conducting the survey fueled the perception that the Americans were seeking to sell their secondhand wares to societies that they thought did not have anything of value to offer of their own. Most politely said that they did not think these products and services developed in the United States were relevant in their market—even if they were to be translated into the local language.

Several years later, still in search of revenue, the association took another crack at the overseas market, but this time it used a different approach. Using the results of a domestic membership needs survey it had conducted, the association approached its sister organizations abroad to ask if any of these findings sounded similar to what they knew about the needs of their own members. For example, its U.S. membership had listed professional standards development, education and training services, and professional networking at a national and international level as the membership benefits they valued and needed most. Indeed, the association learned that the priorities of the members of these overseas organizations were virtually identical to the findings in the United States.

Armed with these similarities in member needs, the association then asked if the sister organizations would be interested in participating in a planning session that would seek to identify those areas that might be in everyone's interest to collaborate in designing products and services that could be of benefit to all. Remarkably enough, the answer was unanimously positive.

A meeting was set, and the planning session, which included the senior administrative and program staffs of each organization, took place in an atmosphere of great creativity and enthusiasm. Participants identified areas of collaboration and international products and services to be developed—such as jointly hosted international conferences and the creation of international standards—most of which keyed off the products and services that already existed at the American association. The association had successfully identified appropriate products and services—not simply putting up "open for business" signs in overseas markets, but by first engaging its international counterparts as partners to learn their needs.

A postscript: unfortunately, in spite of these positive findings, the board of directors could see no value in investing any resources in tailor-making products and services for markets outside the United States. As a result, any international endeavors that might have been initiated have since been stalled.

Perhaps this case sounds familiar? Unfortunately, any number of associations could tell similar stories.

Lessons Learned

Apart from the observations made in the case studies noted above, what lessons can be learned from these examples? Some of the lessons follow:

- *Recognize the need for an international organization.* While there are certainly reasons to be critical of some of the decisions made by players in the International Medical Society referenced in Case Study 3 of the beginning of this chapter, it may not have been in the constituent members' interests to create a global organization—an international organization was more suited to their needs and sense of priorities. The creation of a global organization is not an end unto itself. There must be a practical benefit in store for all stakeholders.
- *Know which services are best delivered where.* In every instance noted earlier, services are delivered at the national level based on such critical considerations as common history, language, culture, regulations, and legislation, not to mention geography, technology, and infrastructure. Governance structures that ignore this reality are doomed to failure.
- *Decide the role of the regions.* Regional structures can serve as useful tools for building a global organization, but as seen in nearly every example, they can also be a distraction, if not a roadblock.

- *Define what constitutes a member.* This is a fundamental question that every organization needs to resolve before it can consider itself a global organization as opposed to a loose affiliation of organizations.
- *Establish funding and financing guidelines.* If an organization depends overwhelmingly on dues payments to operate, it cannot be expected to function as a global entity. Constituent members are going to count what they get in return for what they pay. Members will almost always perceive that they receive less than what they are contributing. Over the short term, reliance on a dues-based budget might work as in the case of the accounting firm but not for long.

  International committee structures as shown in the accounting firm and medical society examples serve as the best tools by which to develop, deliver, and monitor the quality of international products and services provided they are backed by a full-time, trained staff.
- *Know both the language and culture.* For obvious reasons, this is a critical issue for a global organization. Of the examples given here, the accounting firm developed the most successful approach to solving this issue by assigning international staff to the global headquarters.
- *Establish rules for covering travel expenses.* Though another real and potentially crippling issue, all successful global organizations recognize that picking up travel costs for staff and volunteers should be a major part of their budgets.
- *Know your international products and services.* As noted earlier, global organizations must have definable, tangible, and desired products and services. Without these, there is no need for the organization.
- *Determine your paid staff and volunteers.* The number of hours volunteers have to give to nonprofit work is declining. This is a reality in all markets around the world. Volunteers are needed to help define products and services and make key policy decisions, but a full-time professional staff is essential to making things run. Without them, as in the medical society case study above, an organization will wither and die.
- *Establish strategic alliances.* Strategic alliances have their purposes, especially when an organization is small. They help extend reach and economize resources by avoiding duplication of effort. But

strategic alliances are not an end unto themselves. Ultimately, an organization needs to own the turf on which it is operating.

- *Make products that are available and affordable.* Every example here has shown that the volunteer leadership needs to be involved in identifying the products and services the organization offers and ensuring they are adapted and priced for successful use in national markets around the world.
- *Establish the board.* The board needs to be geographically, financially, and intellectually representative of an organization's membership. And if this means it is too large to function efficiently (all the boards noted in the case studies are 15 people or less), then there needs to be an executive committee to ensure adequate control and direction of the organization.

  It is helpful to have a board of officers that alternates between the geographic regions that are most important to the overall membership. It is also helpful to have a vice chair or a vice president who functions as the president-elect of the organization. Having a "former" president position on the board ensures continuity in leadership and may be helpful in avoiding or smoothing over difficulties that arise.
- *Ensure that committees serve the organization's strategic goals efficiently.* Committees are an organization's link to its members and a critical tool for any global organization. But committees are well known for their inefficiencies. As noted in the medical society and accounting firm examples above, some of the more common problems associated with committees can be overcome by:
  - "Institutionalizing" only those committees essential to the organization's mission. The rest should have a defined lifespan, after which they disappear.
  - Defining their objective(s) and holding them accountable.
  - Offering to pay time and travel costs of members in return for carrying out specific "homework" assignments.
  - Providing adequate staff support to ensure follow-through.

Apart from the observations noted earlier, these benchmarking examples illustrate that governance issues are critical to the successful creation and operation of a global organization, but they are not the only critical elements. The other elements include staff, the existence of an overriding purpose, the existence of global products and services, resolution of funding and financing issues, and the simple desire of the various stakeholders to make it work.

Global Localization

Global localization is the term coined by Akio Morita, the late founder of Sony Corporation. While there are many models to follow in building a global organization, you will know that you have arrived when you can say you have achieved global localization.

One day while visiting a supermarket in France, I told the checkout lady that I was happy to find an American brand bar of soap; in this case, it was Colgate-Palmolive. She looked at what I had purchased and observed tartly, "Monsieur, what you have there is not American but a French product!" You know you are global when the local users of your organization's products and services are convinced that you are local to them alone.

One service organization was among the first to develop client-focused service groups according to both industry sector and type of service. Overlapping this matrix organizational approach that included both industry-sector specialization and service specialization was representation according to geographic, national, and cultural origin. So, for example, the organization's banking group was comprised of banking specialists with a variety of skills and who were from a variety of geographic backgrounds—so that when these groups convened meetings they could choose just about any place on the planet and have it equidistant in travel time for all their participants. Although an organization's business may be predominantly in one market, if its structure allows it to shift its focus easily to different parts of the globe, and if a specific geographic location is not central to its identity, then it is a global organization.

A common misconception about globalization is that it is the equivalent of homogenization, or worse—Americanization! While some large organizations are well identified with the United States—such as Coca-Cola or Disney or Levis—their sustained success can be directly attributed to their ability to penetrate and operate in local cultures throughout the world. In some instances, this means adopting local customs; in all instances, it means empowering local managers to run operations in the ways that best work in those cultures, within the well-known principles and fiduciary restraints and responsibilities of the organization.

So what about the American brand identity of these organizations? Does that mean they are less global or that they are handicapped in some way from operating successfully in the global market? Obviously, from the self-evident success of these companies, the answer is no, but what might be less evident is what is most obvious—these organizations have recognized the advantage to their brand image that is offered by having an American identity. Whether you personally agree or not, "America" conveys certain impressions that have positive value and that translate well into brand images for consumer goods and services designed for the youth and upwardly mobile markets of many countries outside the United States. As we will examine later in this book, this strategy can work for associations that are seeking to expand into the U.S. market as well. But don't be deceived by this branding strategy—these organizations are as global as they get!

As a rule, the more global an organization is, the more it is tolerant of diversity. However, the more localized it is, the more the organization must be rooted in a sense of its own purpose and shared global values. This is the glue that holds global organizations together. In effect, values act as a sort of constitution that clearly defines what an organization stands for—for those inside as well as outside any given organization.

For example, we all instinctively know what McDonald's Corporation's values are. If we walk into a McDonald's restaurant anywhere in the world and see that things are dirty, we know immediately that a key value has been violated. Or if we were to order a hamburger and find that it costs $20, we also know something is amiss. In fact, it is safe to say that McDonald's employees, shareholders, customers, and stakeholders throughout the globe know that McDonald's values are cleanliness, affordability, convenience, and family friendliness.

A distinguishing value of Nordstrom's department store is to ensure that all customers walking into their stores leave satisfied—even if Nordstrom employees need to refer them to another store for a product that Nordstrom's does not carry. Similarly, a key value around which L. L. Bean built its success as an outdoor outfitter is that all its customers shall be satisfied with the quality of L.L. Bean's products, or they get their money back. Such values might seem counterintuitive in a business environment. These values cost money! However, the confidence they inspire has led to fiercely loyal customers and stakeholders who truly believe in these institutions.

Values are not goals, but, like goals, they do key off an organization's vision and mission and are in many ways special to that organization.

As can be seen by the McDonald's, Nordstrom's, and L.L. Bean examples values often serve as an organization's competitive advantage in the marketplace. At the very least, the more successful global organizations have a very clearly defined sense of themselves through the values they embrace and incorporate in their day-to-day activities—even as they remain rooted in local culture.

So, as planning groups focus on global expansion, it is particularly important that they ask themselves, "What does our organization stand for and how do these organizational values fit into other cultures?" Some core organizational values can meet resistance in certain local cultures. Wal-Mart's emphasis on "low cost" as a corporate value certainly had this problem in penetrating Germany and Japan—cultures where "low cost" is equated with "low quality." Organizational values do need to mesh with local cultures.

In effect, there are strategic considerations that enter into play that make almost every organization's set of values as unique as a fingerprint and as essential as a heartbeat. Furthermore, these organizational values are not just externally driven; they have internal implications as well, because if they are to be taken seriously, then they need to be ingrained into the organization's culture from the time the first employee is hired in every market of every part of the globe.

Sorting Out What Is Global from What Is Local

This is a difficult issue and one that has been the subject of a great deal of debate and even litigation. Let's start with the easy things first.

Rule 1: Don't do anything abroad that you wouldn't do at home. Just because local laws, regulations, and customs don't prevent you from doing certain things that you would not dream of doing in your home market, don't do it—even if it is cheaper and easier and offers greater short-term profitability. Hypocrisy definitely is understood globally—people know when they are being taken advantage of. U.S. courts are full of litigants from developing countries who have accessed helpful U.S. legal talent that has known how to turn such double standards into a tidy profit for themselves and their clients. But even if you win such trials, you lose in the eyes of public opinion. So companies that have left behind toxic waste dumps in developing countries because they could and companies that have scrimped on safety measures because there were no laws requiring them in certain overseas markets have all paid a price, sooner or later. The axiom in this case is: organizations operating on a global scale have at least two standards that they are accountable to—the local laws and customs of the markets they are in, as well as the laws and customs that they operate under in their home market(s).

Rule 2: Some local customs are more vital than others—but let the people in the local market decide—don't force your will on them! A good example of this is the challenge that Kellogg's had in the 1980s in deciding whether to introduce breakfast cereals into the continental European market that had no such culinary tradition. In France, people ate croissants and rolls for breakfast—the traditional "continental breakfast." In Germany, people ate cheese and sausages for breakfast. So did Kellogg's walk away from those markets? No! But it took them a long time to change these local cultural traditions. They did it in the time-honored tradition—by making it a status symbol that the younger generation sought to emulate. The stodgy, older generation could keep their croissants and sausages—breakfast cereal is the choice of the young and hip! And so it has become. But such strategies are time consuming and costly. This generational strategy took Kellogg's a long time and many millions in marketing to pay off—but pay off it did.

Then there is the case of the Peace Corps volunteer operating in a lesser-developed economy who succeeded in introducing the concept of latrines into communities that had no plumbing facilities. When disease started to break out, the Peace Corps volunteer realized too late that the system he had introduced was actually the source of the problem. The old way he had tried to replace was the better way.

The infamous example of Nestlé selling powdered milk for babies in lesser-developed countries produced similar catastrophic results and cost that company a great deal in prestige and lost sales due to the resulting international boycott of its products.

Some local customs can be changed and others can't. Clear enough? In fact, it is not so clear—either to the global organization that may be entering the local market or even sometimes to the people in the local markets themselves. Suffice it to say that it is enough for those responsible for developing international marketing strategies to know that they need to tread very carefully. Certain decisions may literally have life-or-death implications for the people they seek to serve as well as for their own organizations. Good intentions are not enough. A great deal of thought, time, and research need to be given before introducing any foreign concept or product to a local market. And this also requires patience, openness, and sensitivity to cultural differences and the personality to be able to let things happen. Sometimes new products and uses for old products can result. McDonald's has certain standards and values that they will not compromise, but apart from these, they are very willing to adapt to local market traditions—such as McDonald's in Belgium, a country known for its beer, serving more beer than milkshakes with their Big Macs, and McDonald's in Maine featuring lobster rolls on their menu.

The axiom here? Successful global organizations improve the lives of the people they touch.

Globalization is a fact. It will not go away. If it should, we would all be poorer for it because globalization is nothing more than offering choices. And in each instance, people—valuing what most people value throughout the world—will choose that approach, that product, that style that offers them and their families and friends convenience, status, and a better way to do things than what they had before. Globalization empowers. There are more countries in existence now than at any time in human history. There is less poverty and disease than at any time in the history of the human race. But, some argue, at what cost? Languages are dying out throughout the world, as are many local products and traditions that are quaint but perhaps impractical.

So, unless we can figure out how to convince people to voluntarily turn themselves into museum pieces, people throughout the world will choose what is best for them. And when their choice is made from among many offers from every organization in the world, then you start to see how the power of these choices is shaping the world and those organizations that serve it.

Chapter 3

The Structure of the Globalized Association

There are different organizational options available to associations when faced with some of the strategic and logistical challenges of globalization and global markets. This chapter discusses regional development strategy for associations with limited geographical reach and some of the human resource challenges of managing people across cultures and time zones. It outlines an approach for developing an equitable governance structure that ensures organizational growth. And it concludes with a discussion of the leadership techniques that have proven effective in associations that have become global.

The late Speaker of the House of Representatives, Thomas "Tip" O'Neill, was famously quoted as saying, "All politics is local." Association executives know that all association business is local as well. So how does a U.S. association made up essentially of U.S. members—all of whom have their own local concerns—arrive at the point where it can fashion products and services for the individual needs of overseas markets? Following are two approaches used by two very different organizations.

A Regional Development Strategy

An association of career management consulting firms in Washington, D.C., started in the 1970s as a U.S.-based trade association. This association was made up of domestic outplacement consulting firms that saw the need to develop and impose standards in a relatively new industry plagued by fly-by-night operations that employed questionable business and professional practices. After two decades of successful expansion in the United States, the association saw the need to follow its members' growth into Canada, Europe, and Asia, which had similar needs for highly ethical business standards and practices.

Developing the trade association's presence in these markets proved problematic. Apart from the usual linguistic and cultural differences, the organization was quickly forced to recognize that the employment markets its industry served were different from country to country. Labor laws and practices varied; what was accepted practice or legal in one country was not accepted or was even illegal in another. And because the industry itself was so new, its relative levels of market penetration differed dramatically from one country to the next. Moreover, the global regions that would need to be formed would have a combined annual budget of less than $400,000.

Nevertheless, industry leaders, including CEOs from the most developed markets (North America, Europe, and Asia) came together in a series of meetings to discuss the merits of forming a global organization. While recognizing that each market was distinct in its needs and practices, all saw an overriding need for a global organizational framework through which certain services could be provided. To begin with, participants determined that such services should include opportunities for cross-border professional networking among individuals and firms, recording and exchanging of best practices in ethics and government relations, and creation of a system whereby global standards could be incrementally put in place during the coming decades.

Because the industry was so dispersed and had such an uneven presence in markets around the globe, the leaders determined the best way to foster the global development they sought to create was to build a regional organizational structure, with the most developed national markets in each region assuming a leadership role. Canada and the United States constituted one region, Europe another, and Asia the third. Over time, as the industry expanded and grew in Latin America and Africa, it was envisioned that those regions also would be represented.

Each region would be responsible for developing the services that it wanted for its respective national markets. Further, each region would select its own representative for the associations' board of directors, which would meet twice a year.

The international board, consisting of industry leaders, met to discuss what needs all regions held in common. Each brought to the table what his or her constituencies were asking for so that they could identify common needs and decide whether the association could meet those needs. In doing so, it was able to determine the global services to be delivered and the avenues to deliver them: the Internet (all markets had 100 percent access to the Internet), an annual international conference (to meet the acknowledged common need of networking), and a quarterly global newsletter (to share ideas on effective government relations practices). The association of management consulting firms' website, membership records, and the quarterly newsletter were to be developed and administered by the U.S. office, which was the largest of the offices and therefore had the infrastructure to do so. The content provision and costs for providing these services would be shared proportionately by each of the global regions. The annual conference would rotate among North America, Asia, and Europe. The promotional costs and risks of each conference would be shared proportionately by the regions—according to their contribution—with conference revenues being used to offset these costs. Any profits derived from the conference would be split between the hosting region and the association for use in future programs and activities.

In undertaking these steps, the association of career management consulting firms proved that an association did not have to be large and wealthy, nor does it have to represent a culturally, financially, or legally homogenous industry to succeed in creating such an organization that has global ambitions but with a local focus. In fact, being locally focused, financed, and driven was the key aspect of the associations' success.

Buy-In Through Collaboration

Another example of an organization tailoring its services to international markets can be found in the for-profit sector. In this case, however, it was a matter of bundling services from affiliates in various countries to create a unified global service. In essence, the need identified was to have various local services packaged in the form of a global service. By the end of the 1980s, the Berlin Wall had fallen and the Soviet Union was no more. With the creation of newly independent countries, new markets were opened up, and the rush was on to see which Western companies would be the first to establish a presence there.

For accounting firms, these global developments were a special challenge. Most of these organizations had no presence in these newly opened markets and most did not even have global service packages to offer their clients, who were thinking increasingly in global terms. But globalization was seen as a key strategic advantage to any firm that could structure itself accordingly. The challenges were how best to create a global organization out of a highly fragmented structure and how to enter into new markets where they had no previous presence.

A large international consulting agency in New York City was one of the first accounting and management consulting partnerships to succeed in doing this. The partners of the national practices, which were then only loosely affiliated, determined that building a global organization had to be a priority if they were each to realize the market opportunities that were being presented. The consulting agency's example illustrates the importance of an organization's getting buy-in from affiliates by treating them as equal partners in a global undertaking, as opposed to allowing a dominant member to impose its will on less influential affiliates.

To quantify these opportunities, the various national firms collaborated in assembling a list of all companies in each national market around the world that had an international presence. They then collected the figures of what each of these companies spent in fees for accounting and management consulting services. The sums amounted to billions of dollars—a huge potential market available to those firms that succeeded in developing the global service packages that their current and prospective clients were eventually going to require. Consequently, the national managing partners determined they wanted a global brand image for the firm, supported by global service packages that would be provided by international client service teams. International boundaries would be erased, meaning that one international service team would serve a particular client so that the client would not have to deal with different service teams in different countries. Moreover, the new strategy would standardize quality control across borders; a given company would receive the same level of service in, say, New York City as it would in Paris. Note that the elimination of business boundaries could possibly get sticky, with international teams potentially being viewed as encroaching on the territory of national practices—hence the need to ensure that all national practices would buy in to the global program.

With this end objective in mind, each national practice pledged to contribute a similar percentage of its gross revenue to pay for the effort that would be required in product development and marketing.

The partners assembled a core global practice team, of which I was a member, made up a permanent and seconded staff from the world's major markets, with special concentration on the triad of Europe, North America, and Japan, which accounted for the vast majority of the world's international trade flows. This staff was organized according to the types of global services the partners determined they needed to develop.

The challenge in creating the new global firm was to find those elements of accounting in the local practices that had global potential. In this, the strategy was to develop a client-focused and client-driven firm that could provide global services locally throughout the world.

Committees, made up of senior partners from national practices around the world, met four times a year to make the strategic decisions that were needed to determine which aspects of the various national practices' services would be incorporated into the firm's global service. Significantly, each of the national practices approved final decisions.

Throughout the process, the organization took pains to ensure that sharing of expenses—potentially a sticky issue in collaborations—was equitable. The travel costs of the participating partners were covered by each national practice, and a formula was devised so that everyone paid an equal amount. The travel costs for a group were averaged so that a partner traveling to a meeting from, for example, Australia incurred the same costs as a partner coming from somewhere in Europe.

Beyond this activity, the global coordinating team also sought out market opportunities that the firm as a global entity would try to win. Many of these were new service opportunities with companies requiring global services, but some were for government-financed projects through such organizations as the World Bank and the U.S. Agency for International Development (USAID). Each time the team won a project, new revenues would be generated for each participating element of the global firm—financial proof of the wisdom of this approach.

Today, the international consulting agency stands as one of the world's largest and most successful global service partnerships. It achieved this rank through the effective use of local resources to create global service packages that were greater than the sum of the parts.

As a final note, in spite of the successful global practice that has been created, the national practices have remained strong—perhaps even stronger than the original architects had envisioned, with less business migrating to the global practice than was initially anticipated. One again, this is evidence that products and services must be created to fit the needs of the local market.

Equal Participation

Neither the association of management consulting firms nor the large international consulting agency would have been successful in its international undertakings if it had tried to impose the will of its largest member on the rest of the members. The key to both organizations' success was in their shared global visions that included the recognition that the very differences so many organizations find difficult to accept or comprehend at the local level were in fact the source of their strength. This concept, which is central to American marketing practices, must be applied in overseas markets as well.

Bigger May Not Be Better for Associations Planning to Go Global

Cross-border investments and sales are booming, and all evidence indicates that this activity is growing fastest among small and medium-size enterprises that have obscure names and that make up the bulk of the membership of most associations.

Whereas the international business scene used to be the reserve of an exclusive group of giant companies, for the past five years the bulk of new entrants into the international arena have been smaller, middle-market companies. For example, a recent international survey of middle-market companies (those with annual sales or assets of less than $500 million) showed that 86 percent had sales outside their own country. And another survey of the small and medium-size businesses of the American Business Conference indicated that 24 percent of their total revenue was derived internationally. This same group projected an average compound growth in international sales of nearly 20 percent—twice the rate of most large multinational corporations.

There are many reasons for this development. Capital markets, for example, have been increasingly open to all types and sizes of investors. Today, success is less a factor of size. The most successful companies have a quality product, good marketing instincts, and an adaptive and client-focused management structure.

Given the pace of these changes, "big" may even be a handicap. The priority for most big companies today is to find ways to become as fast and flexible as their smaller-sized competitors. In many cases, it may be easier for younger and smaller organizations to be nimble and to move toward globalization as an entrepreneurial and innovative activity than it is for the larger, older (and slower) enterprises with greater resources.

Clearly, there are many opportunities in the international arena for smaller business members, including smaller nonprofits. There are also a good number of risks, and since small businesses do not have the cushion to absorb the shocks that are inevitable in a trial-and-error method, the key question nagging most of these players is how to minimize start-up risk.

One method of reducing risk is by doing business primarily in developed markets of North America, western Europe, Japan, and parts of the Pacific Rim. Although not growing as fast as Latin America and other regions, these markets are more stable and predictable. Although trade agreements such as the General Agreement on Tariffs and Trade (GATT) and the North American Free Trade Agreement (NAFTA) have minimized international trade barriers as well as linguistic and cultural differences, the effects of sheer distance still represent obstacles to business transactions throughout the world. In a recent multinational survey, small businesses engaged in international trade were asked to list their concerns or needs. The first three concerns were uncertain legislative and business environment, obtaining market information, and finding and obtaining financing.

When asked how they dealt with these concerns, the first three responses given were: they got on the plane, went to the target market, and did whatever they needed to do themselves; they relied on outside advisors; and they relied on government resources. The second response reveals some interesting client-service opportunities for trade associations.

Law and accounting firms have traditionally provided the legal and financial advice and market intelligence that international businesses have required over the years. These professional service firms witnessed events such as the signing of GATT and realized what these developments would mean to international trade and investment.

Few of these firms, however, have known how to capitalize on the growth opportunities of that market sector represented by middle-level and smaller companies. Part of the reason has to do with return on investment.

Most large law and accounting firms are not willing to spend the time or money to serve a "small" client. The question is: from whom do these fast-growing, smaller companies obtain their professional services, advice, and information?

The answers differ from country to country. In Europe and parts of Asia (especially Japan and Korea), if small companies venture abroad, they generally do so under the guidance of their government or national business promotion body.

In the United States, this is usually not the case. For a host of reasons that are not likely to change anytime soon, U.S. businesses often consider their government a hindrance rather than a help. Neither do

U.S. businesses have anything like the powerful Japanese and French national employer organizations to help them compete internationally. Lack of information about financing opportunities, market information, and regulatory and legislative issues is clearly a problem for small and medium-sized business that want to venture abroad—and, as such, these represent potentially valuable new service opportunities for U.S. trade associations to be providing their membership.

Your association has no interest in business outside the United States? Take a closer look. The chances are good that your association's members are not only interested in international trade and investment opportunities, but they are probably already engaged in them! Look especially at your smaller members, since these are the most likely to engage in these practices. It is also the area where your association can make the most difference.

As a trade association manager, the more important question is: what services should your association provide and how can your association best provide them? Concerned that building an international service operation takes more time and money than they have, associations may be tempted to give up before they begin. But as small and medium-size businesses have proven, one does not have to be big and wealthy to succeed in the international business marketplace. Take your cue from these small companies and discover the array of resources that are available to anyone with a desktop computer and modem, and start developing your international networking skills.

Strategic Alliances and Sister Companies

An internal auditors' society in Orlando, Florida, a society for human resource management, and an American society for chemists have all found creative—and different—ways to expand internationally. Following are four techniques that might take your organization down a global path to success.

International Growth: A Look at Four Options

If your organization has expanded or is considering expanding abroad, you most likely have confronted at least two types of strategic issues.

The first issue is structure. How do you position your organization in terms of any sister organizations outside the United States? Are the sister associations rivals or allies? Chances are, they do not fit comfortably in either category. If they cannot be embraced entirely, neither can they be ignored. So what are the strategic options available for structuring your presence abroad?

The second issue is funding. No members want to have their funds used for products, programs, and services that appear to benefit other national markets, so where can you find the funds to create or grow an international organization? And once found, how can you ensure that your members see the relevance of new international activities?

Fortunately, you have multiple options in addressing both the structuring and funding challenges, as the following four examples illustrate.

Networking International Subsidiaries and Chapters. One of the best ways to deal with potential overseas competitors or to provide a seamless global service delivery system for members or customers with global needs is to create a tightly woven subsidiary or chapter network that serves the local market but also is closely integrated into a global operation. One successful example that association leaders should look to for insights is in the corporate world—a global accounting and management consulting partnership.

In the early 1990s, this firm evaluated the economic globalization trends of its corporate market and determined that the best way to attract new customers and avoid losing others to competitors was to create a seamless global structure that could marshal all the resources of the firm's combined operations globally and apply them in creative ways to meet local needs in every national market around the globe.

Transforming a loosely affiliated network of partnerships with different names, cultures, languages, laws, and traditions was no easy matter. But what drove the process was the belief that each aspect of the firm would, in the end, stand to benefit financially. With local clients already in place, the promise of more business through the growing need of multinational clients for integrated global services made it easier to bear the five years of costs and compromises required to create the global firm that it is today.

In this structure each local element is a legal and financial entity unto itself, thus ensuring limited financial and legal exposure for the other parts of the global firm should anything go wrong. Each entity became part of the global organization through the laws of a Swiss *verein*, which is the equivalent of a loosely affiliated trade association or guild through which the members agree to work together in certain ways. Any disputes among these elements were to be sorted out through regional coordinating bodies and, if necessary, the world governing body. Managing partners of the largest firms in each region comprised that global governing body.

It established teams to develop and deliver global services to customers, wherever they may be. This introduced an important new profit-center concept based on global customer service, rather than one rooted in any given national market. The national entities welcomed this, because the global service teams drew on the resources of each respective national operation, and this produced revenue for everyone.

To further fuel the creation of this global entity, they bid on service contracts offered by the World Bank and USAID, which needed accounting, auditing, and managing services in developing markets worldwide. As the firm won such contracts in central and eastern Europe and in the People's Republic of China, it used the new revenue streams to establish national operations in each new market where it had gained a foothold.

The new offices in Moscow, Beijing, and elsewhere were 100 percent funded in the first few years of their existence through the programs they were running for the World Bank and USAID. The bigger goal, though, was to use these contracts as opportunities to find on-the-ground customers who would permit the offices to continue once the international lending agency funding gave out. In every instance, they were successful in doing so.

Developing a Global Federation. Throughout its long existence as a professional auditing society, the Institute of Internal Auditors (IIA) had helped foster the creation and growth of multiple national sister organizations around the world. As it did so, many members of these sister organizations also joined the U.S.-based auditing society.

These developments were mostly positive, but such success created problems of a special kind. Because non-American members paid less for membership than U.S. members, U.S. members of the IIA increasingly complained that they were bearing an unfair proportion of the costs for running programs and activities outside the United States. The non-American members, however, were aware of their own numbers and questioned why the auditing society governance structure was so heavily biased toward Americans.

After engaging all parties in an extensive strategic planning exercise, the IIA developed a federated global structure. National entities remained the primary service providers to their respective national markets; IIA provided services in the areas of networking, certification, and training, and standards development—each of which everyone agreed served widespread need and demand.

The revenues derived from these services constitute most of the funding required to run the global operations. However, to complement these revenues, the IIA also adopted the same strategy deployed by a large international consulting company: bidding on international market development projects funded by the World Bank and USAID. As the IIA wins these international lending agency projects, it generates revenues for the global operation and the national entities that contribute project resources. It also has succeeded in creating new IIA members in these developing markets, some of which have developed their own national organizations.

Such a federated structure has many of the same advantages of a chapter or subsidiary structure but with fewer direct costs and less central control.

Global Strategic Alliances. An American society for professional chemists and a national medical institution are both nonprofit organizations that pride themselves on their American roots, but both also have widespread interests beyond U.S. boundaries. To accommodate the diverse interests and origins of their international participants, both organizations have developed extensive networks of strategic partnerships overseas. These partnerships consist of cooperation and joint venture agreements with a wide variety of other types of organizations to host international conferences and other information exchanges.

Revenue-sharing arrangements are worked out on a project-by-project basis for jointly sponsored conference.

Such alliances offer maximum flexibility to partner with organizations that may share some of the same interests but otherwise are very different. In such arrangements, it is not uncommon to have partnerships with organizations representing governmental and academic entities, as well as for-profit and other nonprofit organizations. Global alliances are easier to put together and even less expensive to operate than a global federation, but they also afford less control or shared sense of purpose than either of the other two organizational types noted previously. Such structures are ideal for nationally rooted organizations that want to remain tied to international trends and developments but that lack the resources or driving incentive to develop permanent operations beyond their own borders.

A Technology-Reliant Global Network. Like most professional societies and even trade associations, the members and board of a human capital society define their interests in terms of their domestic national market. Consequently, it was difficult for this human capital society staff to justify spending more than a nominal amount of time and money on products or services outside of the United States. Nevertheless, this did not prevent the society from developing a model global organization based primarily on use of the Internet.

One found that its sister organizations abroad had a high level of interest in its programs and activities. Accordingly, it developed memoranda of understanding that allowed each sister organization to offer their members access to the society's products and services via the Internet as a membership benefit. In return for offering password-protected access to the members of sister societies abroad, the society also offered to host or link with websites offered by those sister societies in their own languages.

Such an arrangement has constituted a "virtual" global organization for the human capital society and its members while keeping costs to a minimum. In fact, the revenue-sharing arrangements the society has negotiated with sister organizations has produced a modest but positive net contribution to the society's bottom line.

Making the Choice

These four structural examples are not exclusive. In other words, choosing one does not mean you cannot employ variations of other models at the same time. Indeed, it may be possible for one organization to simultaneously use all four models for international expansion at the same time, depending on the opportunities and challenges you may encounter. In effect, these models represent some of the tools available to creative association leaders who recognize the need to grapple with the reality of a global economy.

It is a mistake to think that because an organization is nonprofit, it is not or should not be concerned about making money. While money may not be the end objective of a nonprofit organization, it can be a useful measuring stick for determining the popularity and usefulness of any given activity. In the case of these four models, the revenue drivers come from one or more of three sources—clients, members, or sponsors who have a commercial interest in the success of your undertaking; government funds; and joint commercial ventures in which costs and revenues are split with other organizations.

Not every organization has equal access to each of these three possible revenue streams, but everyone has potential access to at least one. Your only limit to international growth is the one imposed by your own imagination.

Regional Structure, Board Members, and Localization

"What do you want me to do, trust you?" In this era of command-and-control management styles and techniques, it sounds like heresy to suggest that trust might have a place in management; but international management best practices have shown that trust is a critical component to success.

Human Resources—Trust Local Managers to Get the Job Done

Cultural, personality, and language differences, not to mention real and assumed differences in law and business practices, provide many opportunities for misunderstandings, inefficiencies, and missed opportunities. Time and again employees respond to detailed operating instructions from distant managers with a shrug of their shoulders and compliance to the letter—with lackluster results.

However, left to their own devices, local managers, who know the market best, can usually be counted on to find the best way to achieve their objectives. And in the course of doing so, they may also identify new products and methodologies that could have applicability upstream back at headquarters or in other parts of the organization.

Clearly, one of the world's most successful global enterprises, a fast-food hamburger chain, learned early on during its quest to open fast-food restaurants in nearly every country that micro-management tactics weren't an option. For global success, the reigns of responsibility had to be placed in local managers' hands, along with a blueprint for achieving what the company defines as success. The fast-food restaurant developed and implemented a strategic plan with a vision, mission, values, and goals that could be easily understood by every employee. Its vision is ambitious: to have a presence in every community worldwide. Its mission: to feed people. And its values are three: cleanliness, convenience, and affordability.

Within this framework, local managers are given fairly broad operational latitude—including being encouraged to change the menu to fit local tastes and needs. Strict reporting procedures are in place, but apart from that, the world's most successful restaurant chain is remarkably decentralized. Call it trust, but the managers of the fast-food chain restaurant know what is expected of them and are encouraged and rewarded for identifying better ways to get the job done.

You can develop a circle of trust that empowers your local managers by the following:

- Involve them in the association's strategic planning process.
- Encourage them to cultivate and suggest better ways of doing things, through public recognition and performance incentives.
- Share best practices for addressing challenges and creating new ways to realize opportunities.

Remember, trust lubricates relationships and opens channels for creativity and better performance.

Managing in a Global Era: Challenges to Expect

One of the most interesting things about the globalization trends that are shaping every aspect of our economy, society, and culture is how they defy structure. It's almost comical to watch how governments are trying to impose taxing and regulatory and censorship authority over e-commerce and the Internet. Like children chasing soap bubbles, what they are chasing is gone as soon as it is grasped.

This elusiveness of globalization is sure to have a revolutionary impact on both government and management structures that have served us relatively well for the past several hundred years. But with communication and commercial exchanges now happening at the speed of light, how can these antiquated concepts of command and control ever hope to keep up?

The technology that has permitted globalization to happen has unleashed human creativity—for all the good and bad that that implies. It is causing the most sophisticated government regulators to pull their hair out, and business and association managers to be frantic in seeking out new governance models and management tools that will help them tame or at least channel these new tidal changes.

Management models do exist, of course—some of which work better than others—but like most things mechanical, the key to success lies not so much in the machine as in those who are at the controls.

Upon learning that Dwight Eisenhower had won the presidential election, President Harry Truman remarked, "Poor Ike, he will come to the White House and give orders that this or that thing be done—and it just won't happen!"

As powerful as the presidency is, Truman knew, as every president has, that presidential directives can "die of a thousand cuts"—that foot dragging by less-than-enthusiastic individuals can just as surely stop something from happening without outright opposition.

But this is routine for association managers. Volunteer leaders cannot be ordered to do or say anything. Staff members can drag their feet and practice passive resistance. Worse, they can communicate back channel with like-minded volunteers. They and the broader membership's ability and willingness to cooperate on any association initiative depend on the perceived importance of their individual interest level and resource availability. To this extent, the success of an association executive is directly tied to his or her ability to communicate, motivate, and mobilize disparate and quasi-independent interest groups and resources. But this is true with any change to the status quo, not just globalization.

Given the kind of management skill set that has evolved in the association community, maybe the country's leading business schools should be taking leads from association managers as they explore new ways to manage far-flung and fluid organizational structures.

There is another aspect of global organizational management that is peculiar to all U.S. organizations—government, for-profit, or not-for-profit. In a global organization, the temptation to use raw power and force change is even greater than at the national or local level. Not only does the simplicity of this approach have appeal, but most association managers know their size permits them to get what they want, when they want it. In virtually every professional and industrial sector, U.S. associations are far larger and better financed than their overseas counterparts. Why indeed ask when you can tell? Why go abroad when overseas customers, members, or associates can come to you?

When frustrations mount and Europeans, Latin Americans, Asians, or others just don't seem to be doing what they should, the temptation to play the role of the "ugly American" is great.

It is said that the definition of *diplomacy* is "the art of letting other people get your way." It takes a shrewd manager to pull this off, but successful association managers do it every day! Consensus and motivation building are key aspects of the job. And the vital management qualities needed to build consensus and motivation are good communications and listening skills.

Most association managers will agree that strong-arm tactics and turning a deaf ear to member concerns are ingredients in a recipe for disaster, yet it is curious to see how quickly these lessons are forgotten when the people they are dealing with do not live in the United States and may not speak English.

David E. Sanger, an editorial writer for the *New York Times*, addressed this phenomenon in an article, "All Pumped Up and Nowhere to Go" (July 9, 2000). Referring to national governments, he wrote, "to maintain its influence, America must be seen to be sharing power, not hoarding it." This concept of joint decision making and sharing of power or consensus building is very "association-like."

While most associations feel relatively inexperienced in the global marketplace, they can and should take confidence from the fact that the management skills they have honed and that they employ on a daily basis can be ideally suited to the needs of this new global era once cultural differences are recognized and respected.

What Is Fair in a Global Democratic Governance Structure?

"Democracy is the worst form of government," Winston Churchill noted, "except all the other kinds."

For the sake of democracy, associations can undergo some strange contortions in their decision-making processes and structures. Sometimes, trying to do what is right can cause awkward consequences. Do any of the following scenarios seem familiar?

- Popular votes consistently overrule the will of the minority; the only problem is that the minority in this instance contributes most of the association's funding.
- Misunderstandings on a vote cause unexpected questions, complications, and tensions that cause more difficulties than the original question was worth.
- A vote on a controversial issue causes the membership to split into factions that threaten to tear the association apart.
- In a U.S.-focused—or any single-country-focused—organization, these problems usually can be avoided or worked out through rapid, targeted communication and, if necessary, face-to-face meetings. But in international or global organizations—where there are language, cultural, and legal differences, as well as difficulties caused by national pride and simple logistics—such problems are both more common and more difficult to resolve.

Consider the Differences

One nation/one vote may work for the United Nations, but experience has shown that this is a difficult governance model to apply to associations. It is ineffective for international associations to treat their members as if there were no national differences among them. And one nation/one vote ignores the very real differences in size (in terms of both head count and financial contribution) that exist among countries. Therefore, a governance structure must deal with members on a country-by-country basis.

Effectively run international associations recognize that from an operational point of view, member service programs must be supported by national structures. The successful design and delivery of membership services on a global basis depends on a system that is sensitive to the language, cultural, and legal differences among members. Such a structure might include a system of service- or activity-focused committees or staffing structures in which each national constituency is represented.

But for governance matters—where issues of global standards and policies and questions of revenue and disbursement are decided—international associations need to devise a system of weights and balances that can address all of the following real-life scenarios:

- A country accounts for 40 percent of the global membership but contributes 80 percent of the financing for the global organization.
- Another developing country has three times more members than the next largest country but contributes only a small portion of the overall budget.
- Europe votes as a bloc to make it a powerful political influence within the global organization, but is consumed by so many internal needs among its scores of countries (some more developed than others) that it seeks to keep badly needed resources to itself.
- Members from smaller, poorer countries rarely can find the funds to participate in international meetings.

In each of these situations, critical portions of a global organization's membership can feel disenfranchised or "used and abused" unless a fair governance structure is devised. However, most international associations have found that these and other problems can be addressed by finding answers to two key areas of concern: (1) linking revenues to benefits and (2) devising a system of weighted representation that takes into account both head count and financial contribution.

Linking Benefits to Revenues. Money is a sensitive matter and almost always a source of contention. No one likes to pay dues, and almost everyone in a global organization feels that he or she does not get his or her money's worth. The key to avoiding most problems caused by money is to build a structure around sources of nondues revenue. If members want the products and services offered by their global organizational structure, they will buy them. If global products and services cannot be identified, that is perhaps a sign that a large, more centralized global structure is not needed.

Weighted Voting. Most successful global organizations have boards of directors that represent the largest national members, calculated by head count and level of financial involvement. Most also include on their boards regional representatives whose responsibility is to represent the interests of the smallest national members in their respective regions. And most have succeeded in constructing a weighted voting system whereby the strength of a board member's vote depends on the size of the national membership he or she represents as well as the amount of the financial participation in the global organization.

These board representatives in turn are chosen by their national or regional organizations, and travel expenses to board meetings are paid for by the global organization. Board officers are chosen from among the board members and by the board members themselves.

Building a "fair" democratic structure for a global organization takes a great deal more thought, work, patience, and creativity than many might first believe. But, as Churchill would have said, the alternative is much worse.

Leadership in a Consensus-Based Environment

Examples of poor leadership abound in international organizations. They range from leaders so sensitive to each constituent party's opinion that virtually every decision is subject to "death by endless discussion," to leaders who callously push their own agendas regardless of any cares or concerns others may have. In fact, neither of these extreme examples is representative of effective international leadership because neither style is sustainable.

Leadership in an international context embodies the following components:

Vision. Successful international leaders follow a vision that is inspiring, known, and well understood by everyone involved in the organization, both inside and out. Simply put, people know where you are going and why, and they can agree on that—what is better, they are inspired by it! The more widely flung your organization, the greater the need for a vision that can unify all its various components around a purpose that merits the support of all, including direct stakeholders as well as potential outside partners.

Mission. Successful leaders operate organizations whose missions are clear, concise, and recognized as the best or most appropriate way for that organization to realize the vision it shares.

Principles. Every successful leader should embody and respect the founding principles on which their organization is based. These strategic principles or values are what make the organization unique. They constitute, in effect, the organization's binding contract with all its shareholders. This value framework acts as an invaluable point of reference and transcends whatever cultural or linguistic differences that might exist within the global organization.

Strategic principles are sometimes defined as the "glue" that holds an organization together. In effect, these principles or values act as a sort of constitution that clearly defines what an organization stands for both for those inside as well as outside any given organization.

Values are not goals, but, like goals, they do key off an organization's vision and mission and are in many ways special to that organization. The more successful organizations have a very clearly defined sense of themselves through the values they embrace and incorporate in their day-to-day activities.

So as planning groups focus on strategic issues, they eventually always need to ask themselves, what does our organization stand for?

What are the values or principles that are or should be incorporated into everything we do?

There is a distinction to be made in all this talk about values. Personal values are often captured in human resource policies or documents such as employee manuals. Certainly, trust, respect, nondiscrimination (and a long, long list of other values as well) are all part of the personal qualities, ethics, and values that make life livable as well as help to make for a pleasant and efficient work environment. But are they strategic? Certainly, no organization sees an advantage in fostering distrust, dishonesty, discrimination, and so forth.

If it is a given that all these personal values should be incorporated into every work and personal life environment, then what are the types of organizational values that distinguish one organization from another?

In effect, there are strategic considerations that enter into play that make almost every organization's set of values as unique as a fingerprint. Furthermore, these organizational values are not just externally driven; they have internal implications as well, because if they are to be taken seriously, then they need to be ingrained into the organization's culture from the time the first employee is hired.

One would hope that parents and schools have done a good job inculcating the personal values that your organization needs and expects of its employees, but your organization's responsibility is to help these same employees understand what makes working at your organization different from working elsewhere. This, of course, means knowing what these values are in the first place and why they are uniquely important to your organization.

Measurable and Well-Understood Goals

Measurable goals give direction and purpose to an organization and serve as tangible expressions of its mission. Goals also serve as an objective point of reference for evaluating the efficacy of any given effort or program. When an organization's strategic goals are understood, a leader's job is made much easier because then everyone knows what it is he is trying to achieve as an end result.

Is there such a thing as a business or management achievement that cannot be measured? Unless you are a poet or a Zen Buddhist master, the answer is "no." So why is it, then, that so many people who are responsible for developing business plans, strategies, and personnel evaluations resist identifying measurable goals? Don't deny it; it happens all the time—in fact, you may be guilty yourself!

Shall we speculate as to the reasons why people resist measurable goals? Following are some common excuses (along with the possible motivations for each):

- It is impossible to know for sure—as long as we are moving in this direction, why does it matter? (Interpretation: Let's give ourselves some wiggle room so that we can always claim success, even if we fall short.)
- It is simply not quantifiable! (Interpretation: We really don't know what the devil we're doing!)
- Why box ourselves in? We need to allow for creativity! (Interpretation: You scratch my back and I'll scratch yours!)

Do any of these sound familiar?

In our strategic planning exercises with clients, we have found that it takes just as long to identify a metric for a goal as it did to identify the goal itself. It is tough work. Possibly another motivating factor for avoiding metrics is sheer fatigue (or maybe just laziness?) from the mental effort involved in planning.

But plans without measurable goals fail to motivate and guide. Without them, it is simply not possible to manage efficiently and effectively. Without them, management becomes a matter of personality and whim—an environment over which you have no control, unless you are the one at the top! And this, by definition, is a stressful situation.

In our experience as management consultants, metrics are not just for management nerds. Rather, they are the key elements to management success—appreciated by boards of directors all the way down to the lowliest employee.

These four strategic concepts—vision, mission, principles, and goals—provide points of reference that make any leader's job easier.

But apart from adhering to these strategic guideposts, there are personal characteristics as well that good leaders share.

- Good leaders listen well and have cultivated a decision-making process for themselves that consists of thorough research into the facts of a situation before rendering judgment.
- They understand and respect cultural differences and they know what they don't know and can feel comfortable with that.
- They are good communicators. They can make a compelling case—both orally and in writing—as to why people should follow.

Chapter 4

Funding and Financing

Associations must know how to successfully generate the revenues they need to start and to maintain global operations. With enough money, any organization could open offices anywhere in the world. But the chances are that this new structure would not be sustainable because no organization can afford to finance losses for long. Clearly, one of the keys to globalization is finding ways to fund the expenses of the various ways in which associations can operate globally. This chapter discusses funding as a means by which to measure the viability of a particular approach. There are differences between perceived value and cost as viewed by the different stakeholders of any association. This chapter discusses ways and means of engaging for-profit corporations in funding programs, and it discusses effective methods by which to communicate what you are trying to achieve—an effective bridge to the next chapter on language and culture.

Sources of Income

The concept of globalization evokes emotional responses—from the anti-globalization protestors who regularly show up at all International Monetary Fund (IMF)/World Bank meetings to those starry-eyed individuals who seek to create the next brotherhood of mankind. I don't mean to belittle the concerns and aspirations of idealists, but the business of building successful global organizations is as practical as paying the electric bill. Just who is going to pay the staff costs, the computer equipment, the Internet connection, and so forth that would be involved in any such effort? As the following discussions illustrate, costs and potential new revenues are of great concern to your stakeholders, so these considerations need to be front and center in your thinking from concept to implementation.

Generally speaking, there are only four sources of income to fuel an organization's global expansion: your current stakeholders; new members and customers; government, foundation-subsidized, and international development programs; and partnering with sister organizations.

Current Stakeholders

The ticket to globalization for most organizations lies right under their noses—their current stakeholders or members whose own interests are increasingly taking them across national borders. When you are sitting on such an expanding market, you really have no choice but to expand with them or you risk losing your influence and market share to the other organizations they may need to turn to, to serve their expanded needs. Viewed in this light, globalization is almost a defensive strategy. Markets generally are not static. Like a bicycle, organizations have to keep moving—tracking their markets—or they tend to fall over.

Potential New Members and Customers

International markets typically are growing at two to three times the rate of the domestic markets of most developed countries. This has been true since the middle of the 20th century, when the world began rebuilding itself from the devastation of a world war and when burgeoning populations, newly created markets emerging from former colonial empires, inexpensive travel and technology that allowed the easy transfer of people and goods, lower tariffs, and the availability of inexpensive capital all contributed to the greatest sustained period of economic growth the world has ever seen. We, of course, are still living in that period, and along with all these previous influencing factors can be added the creation of new markets due to the fall of the Iron Curtain and the emergence of India and China as economic dynamos unto themselves, as well as the pervasive impact of the Internet as a tool to facilitate commerce. In every instance, associations are finding that growth trends in the sale of their products and services are higher for international as opposed to domestic by a factor of two or three. These figures only reflect trends within the global economy at large. So organizations can choose how they respond—they may choose to do nothing and to operate in a business-as-usual mode, or they may choose to adapt their operations and maybe their program content to better fit the needs of the international markets that offer the best opportunities. Most choose the latter to various degrees; and to various degrees, when they do this, they see a corresponding increase in their revenues. In other words, trimming your sails to catch the globalization winds makes good business sense—it opens new markets and creates new revenue streams.

Government, Foundation-Subsidized, and International Development Programs

Government programs for promoting overseas investment and development exist at both the national and multilateral levels. National programs can be divided into two categories: (1) programs designed to help stimulate international expansion of a country's domestic industry and (2) programs designed to promote economic development in lesser-developed countries. Multilateral government entities such as the World Bank are exclusively the latter. These programs have existed ever since the end of the Second World War and can claim a significant share of the credit for the success of this postwar global economic expansion. More recently, a number of private grant-making foundations have entered the international development arena. While private-sector development organizations have been largely niche players, the hugely endowed Bill and Melinda Gates Foundation is every bit as large and sophisticated in the programs it runs as the U.S. Agency for International Development (USAID)—the U.S. government's premiere development agency. Such foundation work as provided by the Gates, the Rockefeller, and the Clinton foundations have brought a new level of awareness and funding to international development work that has never before been seen.

All these programs, public and private alike, are there waiting to be tapped by associations and professional societies whose standards and credentialing programs, as well as education and training programs, are tailor-made to the skills transfer needs of developing economies.

Partnering with Sister Organizations

Just about every organization can identify a counterpart in another national or regional market that shares a similar or compatible mission. A decade ago it was enough to identify a similar organization in a different market to know that you could work together in organizing international meetings or seminars. This situation has changed somewhat; with proliferation in the use of the Internet, some organizations see their market as being global, regardless of the geographic location of their headquarters. Increasingly, organizations with similar or compatible missions are eyeing each other warily as the potential competitors that they in fact are. Now criteria other than simple geographic location come to bear in determining whether another organization would make a good partner. We see associations partnering with organizations of all kinds—including governments and for-profit companies as well as other associations and professional societies of all kinds and size.

Partnering offers an inexpensive way to immediately become involved in overseas markets, thus extending your organizational reach as well as the diversity of global influences and advantages you can offer your stakeholders. Regardless of the goals driving the globalization of any nonprofit organization, it often makes sense to partner with host country or region organizations, corporations, and governmental entities, since they have the local identity, knowledge, and means to access markets and customers. Regardless of the economic strength and breadth of goods and services of a nonprofit organization, launching a new global membership or product line outside the United States is highly challenging at best. Finding and building successful working relationships with host-country entities is an excellent way to reduce risks and build a successful learning curve. Successful partnering, however, requires a commitment for the success of all partners and for the recognition of the cultures and values of the host-country entities. The best partnering arrangement is one in which mutual respect and frequent communications are matched with the strengths and key experience that each entity can bring to the relationship. Ideally, each participant will bring strengths and opportunities to the relationship that are not otherwise available. Such a relationship results in the whole being greater than the sum of the parts.

Mixed Signals on Globalization

Are you confused or uncertain over the instructions your board of directors has given you about globalization? Don't feel bad. When it comes to globalization, most association executives appear to have a perplexing situation on their hands.

A survey of senior association executives showed that more than 50 percent reported globalization as a "top priority," yet the survey also showed that this globalization mandate has produced few new initiatives. Most of the effects of globalization seem to be limited to greater participation of non-Americans in existing programs and services. These executives also revealed that while their boards recognize the importance of globalization, they do not yet seem ready to invest money in the concept.

It would seem that while the interest in globalization has increased among American associations, not much has changed in budgeting patterns since the mid-1990s, when surveys showed that most associations devoted less than 10 percent—and the major part of these less than 5 percent—of their budgets to international activities. This clearly limits the options available to association executives who may see the opportunities presented by the new global economy but are hamstrung by the lack of resources. Why should this be? There appear to be two reasons.

Association board members may be doing nothing more than voicing members' priorities. Association membership polls continue to indicate that members most relate to associations or professional societies at the local level. National operations are perceived to be far away, and international operations are still farther from their primary concerns and interests. In keeping with Speaker O'Neill's dictum that "all politics is local," association executives know that association management tends to be locally driven as well. If association budgeting is tied to members' interests, as it must be, then it follows that it is difficult to authorize funding for anything that is not locally focused.

This budgeting situation is compounded if there is no tradition for the support of annual budgets devoted to annual research and development—to support new entrepreneurial and innovative activities that keep pace with the changes occurring external to the association. If 100 percent of the annual budget is devoted to annual operations, it becomes very difficult to reallocate funds for something new and untried, such as globalization. Globalization is a challenge to any budget, since it not only is a new activity, but, for success, it must be an ongoing activity for years.

This raises another key point: have the goals and success measures for globalization been clearly identified, communicated, and supported? More often than not, even the best associations can stumble on this essential issue. Why would an association undertake globalization activities? What sort of resources and time commitment will it take to be successful? What are the important success measures? What sort of organizational and marketing effort will it take to best achieve success?

A second reason may be that boards are simply reflecting the ambiguities of American society. Poll results published by the *Wall Street Journal* revealed that only 35 percent of Americans believe that international ties and trading opportunities have helped the United States. In this same poll, 24 percent of the respondents indicated that they felt international ties and trade have not made much difference to the United States, while 32 percent felt the impact to be negative. In other words, those on the positive side of the equation (35 percent) are almost equally balanced by those on the negative (32 percent). Even adding the neutral votes to the percentage of positive responses leaves only a wobbly 59 percent of Americans either positively inclined or ambivalent about international trade—hardly a ringing endorsement for business or association executives to launch new international ventures.

So what are executives to do with the globalization issue when their boards seem to be saying they should push the accelerator and the brakes at the same time? "Best-practice" cases from the association community indicate there are three steps that can be taken.

First, identify and quantify the potential benefits of globalization for your members—and tell your members about them. To gather the information, make use of the U.S. Department of Commerce statistics, information, and anecdotes from members' experiences, and help from sister organizations abroad.

Once all this information has been obtained and analyzed, the next challenge is to explain why it is relevant to members at the local level. This is what Akio Morita, the late chairman of a large electronic company, once referred to as "global localization."

Second, assign responsibility. Associations that have succeeded in leading members into the global arena have hired a staff expert to "internationalize" products, programs, and services by marketing them abroad and making them more accessible to non-American members. Global participation in the association's activities creates revenue streams that are hard to ignore, but someone needs to have responsibility to make it happen.

Finally, you should begin to develop long-term plans that address how your organization will respond to the practical and strategic questions that are sure to arise as (and when) you become more active in the global arena. These global forces that are changing our world so dramatically are most definitely going to have an impact on your organization. Whether this impact is positive or destructive will depend almost entirely on the level of preparation.

The Globalization Dilemma

Those who have the insight and ability to sift through the cacophony of day-to-day living and focus on such history-making developments are the sages of our time. If they happen to be association managers, they also are likely to be the ones whose organizations will be best positioned to thrive in the years to come.

Fashions ebb and flow, but some generations experience trends that have deeper and more long-lasting significance. Few would dismiss globalization as a passing fashion. Although many would and do debate that globalization is a threat or an opportunity, virtually all agree that this is one of those history-changing phenomena that is here to stay. The question is not whether to accept it but rather how to adapt to it.

The regions outside North America where associations saw the most active membership presence were Europe (the region named by the highest number of association executives), Asia (the second highest), and then Latin America. This pattern, with Asia sometimes exchanging places with Europe for the number one position, is a simple reflection in miniature of the overall flows of trade and investment between North American and the rest of the world.

Why shouldn't association executives see globalization as an opportunity for their organizations? U.S. Department of Commerce figures show that the international portion of the U.S. economy (exports and imports) has grown at least two to three times faster than the domestic over the past four decades. These figures for the national economy are reflected in U.S. association membership growth patterns, where overseas membership growth for most associations is twice to three times greater than what they are seeing domestically.

When the notorious bank robber Willie Sutton was captured, a reporter asked him why he chose to live his life robbing banks. His response: "Because that is where the money is!" In this regard, "international" seems to be "where the money is" for associations.

An international business survey conducted by our firm shows that, after membership dues, conferences and trade shows made up the second and third largest sources of revenues for most associations. Given these findings, it is perhaps predictable that the areas of greatest interest for associations when they think of global expansion are membership development, conferences, and trade shows. Certification, education, training, and publications rank lower in this hierarchy—presumably because they offer fewer direct revenue benefits. For most associations, then, the interest in globalization appears to be driven by revenue growth considerations, whether from increased membership revenues or from nondues revenue sales of goods and services to both members and nonmembers.

There is an important exception that needs to be noted. While this finding may be true for the majority of associations, those associations that offer credentialing programs stand out in clear contrast. For associations in the standards-setting, education and training, and publications business, these are usually the largest sources of revenues—far outpacing their membership dues or even their meeting and trade show revenues. Not only are these the largest source of revenues, but such programs are also natural drivers of the associations' globalization activities. Standards—whether product, facility, or professional—act as natural passports for businesses, products, services, and people who seek access to international markets.

What are associations doing to adapt to or position themselves to take advantage of the historic changes brought about by globalization? Apart from translating conference and trade show materials, most associations appear to be set on just making their domestic programs, products, and services available to anyone outside the country that wants to pay for them. In short, they are cashing in on an opportunity to make easy money. But while associations are rounding off their end-of-year finances in this way, many seem oblivious to the opportunities that are passing them by.

As much as a decade before globalization became the subject of street riots in whatever cities the World Bank and IMF were holding their annual meeting, insightful policy makers gave early warning of the problems and opportunities that were coming. The technological advancements and the treaties and subsequent legal and regulatory changes that have facilitated the global exchange of people, ideas, finances, durable goods, and services have created a rising tide for all the world's economies. But while these developments have propelled the world's economy through historic changes and growth, the ride has been rough. Protected or less-than-competitive industries and whole national economies have floundered and are suffering. "Quaint" but inefficient ways of doing things are disappearing. And many have wondered about the fairness of it all. At least one economist has archly noted that in this rising tide "the yachts seem to be rising faster than the rowboats!"

Those who vent their frustrations over these issues by bulldozing a fast-food hamburger chain's restaurant or throwing bricks through the windows of a Starbucks like to place blame on the international bureaucrats and financiers. But they are not listening to what these same bureaucrats and financiers are saying.

The issue of globalization, former United Nations Secretary General Kofi Annan once said, "is primarily one of governance (at all levels)—how the international community of sovereign states and multilateral organizations copes with global challenges, and how individual nations manage their own affairs so as to play their part, pull their weight and serve their peoples."

"It is in our enlightened self-interest to make sure that the losers in this global system—and right now there are billions of them—get a chance to participate," said global financier George Soros.

Michel Camdessus, the former director of the International Monetary Fund (IMF), expressed similar thoughts in a talk in which he pointed out that the problem in thinking globally and acting locally is to "sow the universal at the local level, to plant the universal everywhere. . . . It is in our cities, towns, and residential communities that the global village needs to be built. . . . In this, nongovernmental organizations play an essential role. . . ."

In a white paper developed by USAID, the need to work with and use private, nongovernmental organizations to train, educate, and create lasting infrastructures at the grassroots level in developing and new market economies was identified as being of primary importance.

An organization promoting world health has appealed to private groups representing health care professionals to work with them in developing and implementing programs that will lead to the eradication of whole categories of diseases.

The Geneva-based International Standards Organization (ISO) as well as constituent national standards-setting bodies such as the American National Standards Institute (ANSI) actively seek the involvement of nongovernmental organizations to work with them in setting fair and workable standards for virtually every sector of the world's economies.

Camdessus probably said it best when he pointed out that "the principal challenge of globalization is not to move things around at the top . . . but to develop and solidify its anchor at the local level." And he points out that this linkage, between global decision-making bodies and the grassroots, is best made not by governments but by nonprofit associations.

However, a survey by the Washington, D.C.–based international consulting firm Plexus reveals that standards development, policy development, and education and training do not appear anywhere near the top of the list of what most associations are doing internationally. Why are associations not taking the outreached hand that is being extended to them? There appear to be at least three reasons.

First, there is a lack of self-evident financial interest. If prospective members from overseas wish to join or participate in an association's activities, so much the better—this increases revenues. But the foresighted see that these overseas members may represent the thin edge of a wedge. First they want to participate, and next they want products and services tailored to meet their special needs! But overseas members pay no more—and oftentimes less—in membership dues than their American counterparts; so who is going to pay for the extra costs involved in tailoring products and services to meet these "special" needs?

This concern is most often expressed by boards of directors who are and must be mindful of their association's financial viability. But the professional staffs usually have related concerns. Most association staffs are stretched pretty thin and do not have a lot of extra time on their hands. So without additional income with which to hire more specialized staff to do this extra work, how are they going to cope?

Given boards' concern about finances and staff concerns about serving the needs of a highly diversified membership spread across many time zones, the idea of global expansion often does not go much further. The association's position becomes: "We are an American organization. If prospective members want to participate in our activities and programs, they need to do so on our terms."

The second reason for the apparent disengagement of associations from globalization has to do with governance. As an association's foreign membership grows, staff time and other association resources are necessarily drawn in this direction. This in turn leads to two problems: (1) an American membership that begins to wonder why they are not receiving as much time and attention as they believe they should have (or were formerly used to); and (2) an overseas membership that, realizing the strength of their growing numbers, begin to question why this "American" organization cannot be more responsive to their needs. Non-U.S. members will inevitably begin to feel that more activities should be held in areas where they reside, so as to be more available, with more local content. And if the association is to be credible as a global organization, more and more participation in governance decision making must be available to the non-U.S. members. In this scenario, staff and volunteer leaders and their budgets are caught in the middle.

Finally, the third reason relates to what one association executive calls "the disconnect" between an association's mission and its member services. This comment may seem surprising at first, but it refers to the way members identify with their association. If "all politics is local," the same is true for associations. Membership surveys of professional societies, trade associations, coalitions, and other types of special interest groups consistently reveal that members most identify with their respective groups at the local level. Local chapters are more meaningful to members than national headquarters, and international issues are still more removed from members' practical concerns. Truly successful global organizations must have, by definition, member and customer value-added opportunities at each local level, regardless of region or country. This is much easier said than done, even when these opportunities are consciously acknowledged. This is one of the major disadvantages of the "exporter" or "cross-border" models of globalization that needs to be fully understood by association decision makers.

So what is an association executive to do when members say they want to have their association concentrate on matters close to home and the global economy is pulling in the opposite direction? Or what is to be done if some members are loudly calling for "globalization" as a solution to the declining membership and revenues of an association? Some associations are resorting to technology—delivering and exchanging information internationally through the Internet—and to strategic partnering with sister organizations abroad. These tactics allow associations to respond to the increasing demand for information and services across national boundaries without siphoning off thinly stretched staff and financial resources from their domestic operations.

The demand for these types of services is coming mostly from new markets (such as the central and eastern European countries) or developing markets (such as the countries in Latin America and Southeast Asia) economies where trade associations and professional societies are scarce and, where they do exist, underfinanced and understaffed.

Apart from the concerns noted earlier, once entered into the international arena, most associations are finding themselves faced with four other issues or challenges:

1. Protecting their intellectual property—from both a qualitative and financial point of view.
2. Coping with the inevitable demand for tailoring products to meet local linguistic, cultural, and professional needs.
3. Relating to sister organizations in the more developed national markets that consider themselves equal to the United States in sophistication and that may be leery of a growing American presence in their backyard.
4. Trying not to tread on or otherwise offend the interests of the existing international organizations and governments, where applicable, in their field.

The response of many organizations—to withdraw behind the flag and say, "We are American; the world will just have to deal with us on our terms"—is not an effective answer in today's competitive global marketplace. European and Asian enterprises, for example, often have nonprofit and for-profit organizations that offer similar memberships and access to similar goods and services. Technical knowledge, for example, is certainly not limited to any single country or enterprise. Thus, for success, U.S. nonprofits must see themselves as part of the world marketplace and find their appropriate role as a value-added endeavor.

When it comes to intellectual property, the global arena couldn't be more challenging. Intellectual property is more often winked at than respected in much of the developing world. Furthermore, it is often reasoned that if the Americans insist on being American, why should the Americans care what is done with their products outside of their own country? The products and services of U.S. associations may be admired for their professional polish and sophistication, but many outside the United States feel they should not have to pay to tailor those products to fit local needs and then still have to pay a fee to the United States to use them. Enforcement of intellectual property claims in such cases is difficult and at the very least is a cause of hard feelings.

And what to do about those sister organizations in the more developed markets—like Canada, western Europe, and Japan? Organizations in many of these markets frown when their U.S. counterparts become overly active in what they consider to be their turf. Furthermore, many have products and services that might be every bit as sophisticated as the U.S. products. When differences occur, as is often the case, the question then becomes whose products, services, and standards will dominate the global marketplace? With Canada more often joining the United States, and Japan remaining discretely on the sidelines, transatlantic tugs of war are becoming common for virtually every economic sector. Inward-looking U.S. associations tend to be bypassed and not to do so well in this competition.

Finally, there is a clear reason to feel awkward when dealing with international bodies that are more often than not underfunded and understaffed. And when U.S. organizations participate in such bodies they feel like Gulliver in the land of the Lilliputians! Moreover, most of these organizations have UN-like governance structures that promote the concept of one country/one vote. In such cases, the U.S. member organizations often find themselves the only ones able to finance the initiatives that come out of these deliberative bodies. Too often, their mandate from the membership is: "Please pay, but keep your opinions to yourself!"

Association staff members see all of this up close. They are usually very much aware of the problems and possibilities of globalization. More often than not, professional staffs see the global mission of their organizations but feel restrained by their U.S. roots.

From a global perspective, it may seem trite to affirm that the world needs the participation of U.S. organizations—but it is nonetheless true. U.S. science and industry are on the cutting edge of sophistication. U.S. organizations are generally well run and have the financing and staff to produce products and services that are the envy of the world. But does this mean that U.S. organizations can sit back to wait for the world to come to them, on their terms? Most definitely not. In a dismaying but growing number of cases, U.S. organizations are being bypassed by organizations from other nations that have mastered the ability to form and to lead global initiatives. These are the organizations with which the UN, the World Bank, the ISO, the World Health Organization, and the other global policy-making bodies are working.

But there should be no illusions; individual Americans are participating in such initiatives—it is just that they are not doing so by means of their own, U.S.-based organizations.

It used to be that the brain drain always worked in the United States' favor. But if U.S. associations are to retain their best and brightest members and to play a meaningful role in the new global economy, their professional managers are going to have to develop ways of grappling successfully with the dilemma of globalization—implementing global concepts at the local level while fostering an appreciation of the importance of local concerns on a global basis.

Moving from Corporate Sponsorship to Corporate Partnership

In the United States, nonprofit and for-profit organizations have long been considered uncomfortable bedmates. Associations may actively seek corporate sponsorship dollars or otherwise offer corporations a means by which to participate financially in their activities even while being protective of the level of influence these companies may want to exercise over their program content. To corporations, this sensitivity might look like associations are saying: "Your money is welcome; now please go away!" And in many cases, this is not far from the truth.

But keeping for-profit corporations at arm's length is proving increasingly difficult. Like it or not, traditional lines between for-profits and nonprofits are blurring. For one, corporations increasingly see the value of doing well by doing good. It is common now to see corporations incorporating green technologies and social causes into their everyday business practices. But more than this, corporations are also taking interest in the profitability of certain work that used to be the exclusive domain of nonprofits—particularly in the fields of education, training, and credentialing.

What are associations to do in such an environment? Some have found the answer lies in partnering. Partnering, as defined in *The Power of Partnership* (2008, ASAE & The Center), is "a cooperative agreement between two or more organizations where involved parties share the profits and/or losses of the activities they undertake. The term partnership, therefore, implies that both parties can benefit if the relationship succeeds—and both partners may lose something should the relationship fail in some way. They share risks equally."

This may be a novel concept for associations that are more used to viewing for-profit companies as either arm's-length sponsors or market rivals, but partnerships between the two are increasingly common. In fact, according to *The Power of Partnership*, 73 percent of companies say that partnerships with nonprofits and other socially responsible organizations will be important in the next three years.

Usually—but not always—for-profit companies are motivated to partner with nonprofits to generate profits. The same, of course, could be said of the nonprofits' motivation. Another motivating factor is public relations and marketing purposes: the nonprofit lends credibility to a program or event sponsored "for a good cause" by a for-profit company. Managed carefully, such partnerships can reap promotional value for both partners.

Similarly, for-profits and nonprofits may partner in the name of social responsibility—being a good corporate citizen. Some of these initiatives may flow from state and federal regulations, such as the Community Reinvestment Act (CRA), which requires financial institutions to reinvest in their local communities. But increasingly, for-profit corporations recognize that in doing well by doing good they have a natural advantage in working with those nonprofit organizations that already have access to target audiences, a delivery structure in place, and credibility within the community.

Private interest and the public good need not be in conflict, and nowhere is this more evident than in the growing number of association–for-profit partnerships that have been and are being developed.

Any organization can lose money; the key to successful organizational globalization is to create a means of delivering products and services that is sustainable—meaning that the initiative can cover its own costs and grow of its own accord, fundamentally, because it responds to the needs of the market.

Is Your Organization Ready?

It is not a coincidence that some organizations always seem to have some interesting initiative in the works. How do they do it? Some organizations may have their own significant financial resources to draw upon, but no organization is wealthy enough to do everything everywhere. So, how do the high-performance organizations manage? Simply put, these organizations know what they want to achieve and they have marshaled their resources in a way that ensures they get there in the most effective and efficient ways possible.

The first step is gathering reliable data and turning it into intelligence. What do your markets or potential markets abroad need, and how can your organization respond to whatever opportunities or threats there may be? Too many organizations make decisions based only on gut instinct or through simply following the private agendas of their largest or most influential (or most vocal!) members, as opposed to making decisions based on the facts of any given market. As a result, such factless, purely political decisions almost always result in disasters of one kind or another. The best way to avoid this is to engage professional market researchers in the task of mapping the terrain of your target markets with statistically valid findings derived through a variety of research techniques. The purposes of such research are multiple and can encompass:

- Identifying what your current and potential market needs are and which, if any, organizations are currently addressing these needs.
- Measuring your organization's comparative strengths and weaknesses in each market and market segment.
- Identifying laws and cultural issues that may hinder market penetration or perhaps alter your approach, and if you do such surveys on a regular, periodic basis.
- Identifying and tracking trends so that you know where the market is headed as opposed to where it has been.

You can also use a variety of qualitative research techniques to test ideas and approaches to see what will work best for you as well as what may have worked or not for other organizations facing similar challenges and issues on a market-by-market basis. There are costs in doing this, of course, but the resulting market intelligence is invaluable and can save a lot of the pain and suffering associated with the "ready, fire, aim" approach of more politicized, more impulsive, and less prepared organizations. This approach will guide you toward your current possibilities—the "low-hanging fruit."

As a second step in your research, you may want to look outside your current markets to determine what potential might exist in those areas where you may not have ever thought to have a presence. Identifying and weighing the potential in totally new markets is more difficult when you do not have any members who are familiar with the terrain, but the fact that you do not now have a presence doesn't mean there isn't great growth potential that you might be overlooking.

There are a host of quality market research resources available to the public and more become available through the Internet each year. National (some national governments are better than others at collecting up-to-date and accurate market data) and multilateral (such as the Organization for Economic Cooperation and Development, better known by its acronym OECD) governmental bodies collect and maintain economic data depositories on global markets that are gold mines for market researchers.

The questions you should be seeking answers to in this secondary research are:

- Is there real or potential market demand for the types of products and services your organization has to offer?
- If so, how are these markets currently being served?
- Are the organizations currently serving these markets potential partners or dangerous rivals?
- Are the laws of these markets amenable to foreign entrants? What has been the track record of success or failure of other international organizations that have sought to enter these markets?
- Are there cultural prejudices that would necessitate different strategies or that might preclude entry altogether? What has been the experience of related or similar organizations operating in these markets?
- Is there anything about these markets that would cause your organization to operate differently or that would require a different approach to governance than in the other international markets where you are currently established?
- Who are the members/corporate/public sponsors who would most likely play a lead for you in developing these markets?
- How do you prioritize these markets, starting with those that are easiest to penetrate and that offer the greatest return on investment—short and long term?

Your secondary market research ultimately needs to be backed up by primary market research using whatever means available to you (the best tactic is to identify knowledgeable individuals who agree to be interviewed) in each market to confirm what you have found and to flesh out the details for approaching those markets that seem to offer the most return on investment.

Develop the Program that Matches Your Organization's Needs

One of the biggest mistakes organizations make is to pursue a certain organizational or governance structure without having first considered the types of membership or products and services that these various global markets want and that the organization has the potential to deliver in a cost effective way. These members or products and services are typically the lifeblood of an organization and need to have the structure and governance support that will allow them to grow and thrive. Without this link, organizational and governance structures have no redeeming value.

Form follows function. For example, an organization whose growth is driven primarily by a global credentialing program is likely to be highly centralized, with little need for employees and a brick-and-mortar presence in each global market. However, an organization that is driven primarily by locally delivered services such as lobbying or professional training and networking events will indeed have a need for an on-the-ground presence in each market.

Developing on-the-ground presence in foreign markets can be both costly and risky, but this is not always necessary. The fastest-growing organizations have mastered the ability to find and develop strategic partnerships that build on existing infrastructure and relationships in any given market. Such arrangements allow instantaneous penetration of new markets without onerous start-up or heavy overhead costs. Although the up-front costs and attendant risks are less, identifying, forming, and managing such partnerships are tricky. One study published in the *Harvard Business Review* found that approximately half of all partnerships end in failure, as defined by the partners themselves. What can you do to ensure you are on the winning side of this 50:50 win-loss ratio?

As in most things, preparation is the key. The first step is to spell out your exact needs, then match them with any and all organizations—public or private—that fit the bill, or that come close. Once you have developed this list of potential partners, you need to study each to see how their strategic plans match your own—do they in fact have compatible or complementary visions, missions, and goals? How do their organizational value structures and business styles fit with what your organization is comfortable with? And, finally, what compelling reason do they have to be interested in what you want to propose?

U.S.-based business interests tend to move quickly in identifying, approaching, and contracting with potential business partners, but most of the rest of the world is more deliberate. In most markets outside the United States, prospective partners take the time to develop an understanding of each other before forming any serious commitment. They appreciate that hastily formed partnerships are just as quickly dismantled and that, when that happens, something important is lost in the process.

It is prudent to always give careful consideration and do further research before approaching a potential partner abroad. For example, do you know the real decision makers there (these may be different from those who hold the titles that may be familiar to you), and how they make their decisions? Who within your own organization or within your circle of acquaintances might know someone in the other organization who can give you insight into their language and culture, as well as their personalities and processes? Time and effort spent in such preparation can save enormous headaches later!

In forming an agreement, it is important to draft a written document that spells out each party's expectations. This should include answers to the following:

- What is each party's goal in this partnership and within what time frame?
- What are the intermediary steps that need to be taken to get to those goals and within what time frame and using what resources?
- Who is the person within each partner's organization who is responsible for managing the partnership? Are these responsibilities part of their job description, or do they interfere with their day-to-day responsibilities?

- What resources is each organization contributing, and are these in proportion to the value of the goals that are expected to be achieved?
- How will communications between the organizations be handled? How frequently and by whom?
- If the people handling the project are not the CEOs themselves, then how will the CEOs be involved? Scheduling periodic, face-to-face meetings of the partnering organizations' CEOs is critical in ensuring that each organization stays on track in delivering what they have committed to do.
- If the intermediate steps are missed, causing achievement of the goals to be put in doubt, how do you close down the partnership? How are incurred costs to be covered or losses shared?
- Alternatively, if the partnership is more successful than originally foreseen, how will these additional revenues, or credit of any kind, be shared?

Managing the Relationship

Even the best-conceived partnerships cannot run on automatic pilot, as countless things arise during the execution of any plan that are difficult if not impossible to foresee. This means that you not only have to have a written plan to articulate what you want to do and how you expect to do it; you also need a decision-making and communications structure that can track progress and gather and assess information, and that can incorporate changes into your planning as and when changes are needed.

The best management structures are nimble and in a constant state of readiness. They are also backed by internal management support that can ensure people are paying attention to what needs to be done and that they have the resources available to them to do their jobs.

Successful Leadership Characteristics

When a friend pointed out to him how difficult he was for other world leaders to deal with, Charles de Gaulle, the notoriously prickly president of France, responded astutely, "It is because I am too weak to bend." As a rule of thumb, the more powerful your position, the softer your touch should be in the international arena. No one likes a bully, no one likes to be brow-beaten into submission—the strong don't have to take it, but actually neither do the weak because without the support of even the weakest, initiatives can and do die from a thousand discrete cuts. It is a cliché, but true, that the best leaders lead by example. They also are conscious of and respect the many complexities of international markets and international transactions generally—they know what they don't know.

Leave Your Cultural Mind-Set and Assumptions at Home

In a public works project in a North African country, the government put out a request for bids for the purchase of heavy construction equipment. The competition came down to two firms—one from the United States and the other from France. The Americans knew they were on French turf, as the country was a former French colony; nevertheless, they felt they had the advantage because not only were they offering what objectively was superior equipment, they also knew their price was so low that the French company could not possibly beat them.

So, guess who won? The French bidder, but not because there was any anti-U.S. prejudice or because there was any corruption per se. The French company won because they had taken time to fully understand everything about the decision-making process. They had found out that the decision lay essentially in the hands of one person and that that person's compensation was directly tied to the value of the contracts he presided over. So the relatively high price of the French bid actually served as an incentive for the government official to choose the higher bidder—regardless of which one it was. It was a fringe benefit that the official could actually speak to the French in their own language because he had gone to school in France. The Americans never knew what hit them.

This case illustrates the importance of humility and of taking the time and making the effort to research the local market and of not making assumptions based on the ways things may be done at home.

Foreign language ability helps a leader function effectively in an international environment, because along with learning a foreign language comes an awareness that people literally think about things in different ways according to their culture. This is not necessarily either "bad" or "good," just different. So you might not know the language of the particular market you are in, but if you have had the experience of learning any foreign language, then ideally you are sensitive to critical cultural nuances that might go unnoticed by those who have not had that education.

Be Generous in Sharing and According Credit

For this reason, prima donnas and highly controlling personalities tend not to do so well as international leaders. President Ronald Reagan kept a plaque on his desk at the White House that said: "There is no limit to what you can accomplish if you don't mind who gets the credit!" Being prepared to share and award recognition is a tremendously effective way to win friends and influence enemies across all sorts of cultural barriers. And in this same vein, management by objective works better in an international context than prescribing every detail about how things should be done. Unless these details are truly an essential element in the picture, allow people the flexibility to do things their own way and you just might be surprised at the creativity and innovation you have unleashed. If they are open to it, organizations that operate internationally often find they learn as much or more than they teach abroad.

Use Images in Communicating Your Message

Walking through the souk in Marrakesh, Morocco, I saw dozens of people sitting in circles on the ground surrounding speakers who were variously sitting or standing while keeping eye contact with their audiences and gesturing vigorously. Some circles were dominated by children, who would laugh and squeal at what they heard, while other circles were dominated by sober, intent adults. Some circles were large and some were small. I asked our guide what all of this represented. "They are storytellers," he said. "Each circle represents a different story being told, and whether a circle is large or small is a reflection of a storyteller's abilities." This is the Marrakesh version of American TV channels—only if you want to change channels in Marrakesh, you move to another circle!

Storytelling, of course, is not particular to Morocco; don't we all remember as children having an adult read a story to us at bedtime or even perhaps during the day if we were lucky? Perhaps you have passed this tradition on to your own children with the same spellbinding effect.

What is it about hearing stories that fascinates us? Perhaps it is in our genes. Perhaps Darwinian selection winnowed out all those humans who would not or could not listen to what they were being told! Regardless of the cause, in the end we all like a good story. Stories appeal to both sides of our brains—the rational and the emotional—and the result is that we can often easily recall the details of the stories we were told decades after the fact.

Storytelling transcends cultures, languages, and generations. It offers an almost magical way of capturing attention and creating a lasting impact. Come to think of it, what a wonderful communications technique this is!

As we who are or have been involved in corporate communications concentrate on boiling down messages to "just the facts"—terse little, forgettable sound bites—maybe it would behoove us once in a while to go back to our childhood roots and find what we need to put our messages into the form of a good story. Who knows, you might end up creating messages that people remember a generation from now!

Chapter 5

Language and Culture

Irish writer George Bernard Shaw famously wrote that the British and the Americans are two peoples divided by the same language! We English speakers all know instances where this has proven true—but what happens and how can we cope when the language and cultural differences are truly great? This chapter includes case studies of successes and failures to illustrate what works and what doesn't in a multicultural and multilingual environment. It discusses cultural differences on the critical issue of intellectual property rights and the strengths and liabilities of using and relying on local representatives who speak your language. And, finally, it discusses those cultural traits that are universally respected and value strategies that work across national borders.

Cross-Cultural Deal Making: Don't Take "Yes" for an Answer!

"But our meetings were positive—we actually had bought our plane tickets to attend the final session in Paris, where we thought our agreement was going to be signed. We called to confirm we were coming and were told there was no need! The agreement is off, and we don't even know why!"

Have you ever found yourself in a similar situation? Many Americans and others from classic low-context cultures occasionally do. When international deals go bad, the temptation is to dismiss them as examples of the "perfidious French" in action or the "sneaky (fill in the appropriate nationality) showing their true colors!" By the way, what is a low-context culture, anyway?

Lows and Highs

Those who've taken international marketing courses are perhaps familiar with the differences between low-context and high-context cultures. The United States is considered a *low-context culture*—we try always to say what we mean and to do what we say, and we appreciate this straightforwardness in others. All English-speaking countries tend to be low context. And as businesspeople who are the products of a low-context culture, we find it entirely possible to work with total strangers—and frequently do. If we have the right agreement, with the right terms and conditions, we shake hands and "do the deal" or turn it over to the lawyers or staff "to work out the details." It's even possible to do all this in a single meeting. In fact, it is good when we can do our business quickly, because "time is money." If anything should go wrong in a deal, we just bring the lawyers back in to straighten matters out and we "move on."

High-context cultures, however, are more numerous throughout the world. Most of continental Europe is high context, as is Japan. The Japanese are famous for smiling and saying "Hai (Yes)." But most American businesspeople have come to know that this doesn't necessarily mean their Japanese counterparts are agreeing with them. Rather, they're acknowledging that "yes, I hear what you are saying."

In high-context cultures, business deals are most often struck among friends, family relations, and other close associates. Strangers usually do not succeed in this environment, and lawyers don't have much of a role to play in cultures where verbal agreements and understandings are often considered more serious and binding than written contracts. In truth, they are more binding because personal honor and integrity are at stake, and these are qualities that are valued more than money—don't make the fatal error of believing otherwise.

Dancing Lessons

Meetings in high-context cultures can be frustrating and puzzling affairs for an outsider from a low-context culture. Meetings often start with what Americans call small talk:

- "Are you married?"
- "If you have children, what are their ages?"
- "Do you play sports or have any hobbies?"
- "Where did you go to school?"
- "Where does your family come from?"

Age, gender, and title play important roles. A 35-year-old wunderkind may be surprised to find she is having difficulty establishing simple eye contact with the older man across the conference room table.

In high-context cultures, such get-acquainted rituals have a purpose: to help executives evaluate whether you as a stranger should be granted access to their inner circle. The fact that you are having this first meeting means you have established some level of credibility, but whether you are invited back depends on much more. Such follow-on considerations might include:

- Are you trustworthy?
- Do you take them and the business you are discussing seriously?
- How important is this business relationship to you?
- Are you in for the long term?
- Will you be there for them tomorrow if and when they should need you?

In slower-paced high-context cultures, quick deals are unheard of. This is their business you are discussing. More than likely, the leaders have spent their professional lives developing this business, and they expect to spend what remains of their useful working lives continuing to build it. So if you want their cooperation, you will have to deal with them on their terms, or you won't have their business—it's as simple as that.

Listening to What's Not Spoken

Now back to the case of the canceled meeting in Paris; there is, of course, more to the story. The first meeting went well and led to a follow-up meeting. The Americans viewed the second meeting as the time to set the terms of the deal. Despite having to work through a French interpreter, they got down to business fast and defined all the terms of the arrangements quickly, and in as much detail as a single day would permit, before heading back to the airport and home. The third meeting, in the Americans' minds, was a formality—one in which the deal would be blessed by a broader group of directors. But, of course, the third meeting never happened.

The Americans thought they had the elements of a deal after the first meeting, and they undoubtedly did, but did they still have an agreement after their second meeting? They left the latter thinking they did, but they were completely missing the signals being sent in a high-context culture.

If this is yet another case of low-context businesspeople not being in sync with the values of a high-context culture, how can such problems be avoided? Here are some thoughts to consider:

- *Do your homework.* Use every reliable source to find out about the people and organization you intend to deal with. Who are they, what are their needs, how are decisions made, and can you tailor what you have to say in a way that will be received best?
- *If you don't have the time to research the people and organization yourself, delegate it to a person who does.* Use the best-qualified person in your organization that has time to devote to the project and experience with international/intercultural negotiation, or hire someone who does. Make sure they have ample resources. Make yourself available at the end to sign the deal, but do not engage yourself up front if you do not have time to follow through.
- *Try not to rely on a translator provided by your prospective business partner.* Ideally, you should speak the language or, if not, employ someone who can speak for you. Interpretation from one language to another is not a science but an art. Do not allow yourself to be tone deaf to nuances, gestures, and expressions that may mean a world more than the actual words used to translate them.

- *Think long term.* You may be a person who is going places quickly, but if you want this international agreement, you need to think long term and be able to express what you want in terms of years and decades—nothing shorter is going to be considered as a serious proposition.

There is nothing wrong with being from a low-context culture—except in not being self-aware that your culture and approach doesn't work everywhere. Sometimes, you cannot take "yes" as an answer.

Language and Policies Relating to Languages

Some people are born with finely attuned social skills. Such people can pick up on signals projected by another person's body language or voice inflection; and this gives them a natural advantage in learning to function in an international environment—whether or not they actually speak the language in a given market. Opposite this type of person are those people we all know who are "tone deaf" to nuances and need to have things clearly and loudly spelled out for them. So while it is hard sometimes in interviews to tell whether a person fits into one category or the other, one of the skills that is easy to verify is whether a person has learned and is fluent in a foreign language. If anyone has spent time studying and ideally mastering a foreign language, you can be fairly certain they have learned to understand the sometimes subtle difficulties that language and cultural differences can present. Organizations that operate internationally need for their managers to have such skills and you can pay dearly in ruined or missed opportunities if they do not.

Lacking such basic skills as being able to speak the language of the market you are in makes it incumbent on you to hire a person who does—ideally as a full time part of your staff or, if you are just contemplating entering the market and are not ready to hire, as a one-time contracted professional interpreter. These people can and should be able to tell you the unspoken signals they are picking up from your counterparts as well as what was spoken. They can also advise you as to the cultural do's and don'ts when meeting people for the first time and in setting up and conducting your negotiations.

However, some organizations can go overboard when it comes to languages. Taking their cue from the United Nations or the European

Union, some organizations take it on themselves to translate their materials into every language where they have or wish to have a presence.

This is a thankless task and a very expensive one. Did you know the majority of people employed by the institutions of the European Union are engaged in translating documents? It is thankless because translating is more of an art than a science. Fortunately or unfortunately, there is not just one way to say something. The words chosen, the context, expressions, and phraseology all differ to a greater or lesser extent from person to person and especially from culture to culture—even when everyone is using the same language. Well-intentioned organizations find themselves tied into knots trying to hit the subjectively different and changing targets that translated documents vainly try to describe for local readers. Apart from the time and expense, this issue becomes even more serious when one considers the legal ramifications—which language version of your documents have legal status when there might be differing interpretations of what is stated? Such issues can create a lawyer's paradise of problems!

Since the beginning of the 21st century, the international language of the world has been English. Every international organization recognizes this and has factored it into their business models. It is a factor in deciding whom to promote into senior management positions and it is a factor in preparing for every meeting—whether in person or virtually by Internet or satellite link-up.

As a courtesy to the local market in which an international organization is holding a meeting, the conference language may be in English, but simultaneous interpretation services are usually also provided for speakers of the local language. Otherwise, participants are on their own to fend for themselves in English or to pay for their own interpretation needs.

As and when international organizations do provide translation services (*translation* most commonly refers to written documents, while *interpretation* refers to the spoken word), they usually have designed and adhere to rules that are known and agreed to by all their stakeholders. These rules might read as follows:

- The official language of the global organization is English, but the only documents having legal status in that language (for our organization) are those approved by the headquarters general counsel's office.

- Documents used strictly for a national market whose language is not English may be prepared at the local chapter office's expense and with the review and approval of headquarters. (Remember always that you are responsible for any documents that may put the worldwide organization at risk legally for charges of fraud or defamation or any of a number of issue areas where litigants might find it of interest to press damage charges against the organization's headquarters—because that is where they know the money is!)
- Other documents containing the organization's intellectual property that is sold commercially should be made available locally in whatever language is desired—as long as there is enough of a market to at least cover translation and printing costs. The best way to address the cost issue, as well as to address the specific language needs of that market, is to enter into an agreement with the local entity that they take on the responsibility of translating and printing the document(s) themselves (with approval from headquarters on the final version) in return for the full proceeds from the royalties on subsequent sales, that would normally be paid back to headquarters, to be kept in country for two years or as and when their translation and printing costs have been covered—whichever comes first. This arrangement might cause the local office to think twice before committing to translate documents; it also incentivizes them to promote sales of your organization's intellectual property in an equitable and expeditious way.

Guarding Your Intellectual Property Rights

Your organization's intellectual property is its lifeblood. It is most probably what caused your organization to come into existence in the first place, and it is what keeps your organization alive. It is also what will power your growth globally. Products and services can be made and delivered anywhere, but the ideas that underlie them all belong to someone somewhere. The people and their employers that produced these ideas should be the beneficiaries of the value that they have added. Sounds simple, doesn't it? Well, there is a reason that intellectual property law is one of the fastest-growing disciplines throughout the world. It is on this battleground that the winners and losers of globalization will be determined. What? You didn't know you were in a fight? Look again.

One U.S.-based association that develops and sets professional standards had long considered markets outside the United States to be of minor interest. They did not give much thought to an Indian entrepreneur who approached them to ask for membership along with copies of all the products they could give him. Years later, after this organization started to open its eyes as to the possibility of international markets—particularly the world's largest English-speaking market, India—they found out, much to their surprise, that their logo and products were enjoying significant use throughout India! The Indian entrepreneur had become very wealthy as the self-appointed representative of the association in that market! Winning the rights back from this Indian businessman through India's courts of law proved to be a time-consuming and costly process.

Unfortunately, such cases are not uncommon in the world's developing markets—precisely the markets that are growing the fastest for the sorts of professional and product standards and the training programs that accompany them that are being developed and sold by associations based in the West. Lest we be too quick to condemn piracy of this sort, Americans should take a look at how some of our own early industries got started in the 18th and 19th centuries. Our hands were not too clean then, either!

Nevertheless, intellectual property theft is a crime that is more or less punished around the world, but detection of the crime remains in the hands of those who own the property to begin with—you cannot expect foreign governments to do that for you. Governments may wink at infractions, but under an international treaty that is enforceable by the World Trade Organization and through bilateral trade agreements, these governments are obliged to enforce the law that protects intellectual property owners—if violations have been found.

This last point is key and one that illustrates why no viable commercial organization can opt out of the global economy without potentially fatal consequences for itself. It matters not whether you choose to expand into global markets. Those same global markets will be coming to you sooner than you may think if you possess anything at all that has commercial value. You may choose not to be a global player as easily as you may choose not to breathe. In other words, you really don't have a choice!

How does an organization do this if it does not have plans to expand abroad? It is easier than you may think. Every organization should do periodic Internet searches using their own names and logos as well as their product names—just to see who, if anyone, might be using them around the world. You might be surprised at what you find! For this same reason, it also pays for organizations to maintain contact with sister organizations in other countries. Let them know who you are and what you do and try to keep informed of their activities as well. This may lead to opportunities for collaboration. At the very least you will be developing a worldwide network of people to help you monitor and protect the commercial use of your name and products. Sometimes the best offense is indeed a good defense!

Should Your Brand Be Scrubbed Clean of Any Cultural Bias?

Being from a particular country is not necessarily a bad thing. The French have long played on the image of France as a country of suave romance, fine foods, sophisticated wines, and *joie de vivre* to give their products a certain "cache"—not to mention a higher profit margin! Levi Strauss is a successful global company, but it has built its business around the image of its origins in the 19th century as a company serving the rugged clothing needs of the "Wild West." So while Levis are made and sold all around the world, the tough and independent U.S. cowboy image remains, and this has served the company well in its successful expansion into every market around the world.

However, some organizations do seek to divorce themselves of their origins in order to be seen as a more purely global entity. The California-based express delivery company DHL is an example of one company that pulled up its U.S. roots and moved to Europe, where it perceived it could operate more effectively as a global company.

Such decisions are all legitimate choices that relate to branding and marketing strategies, but when it comes to governance, human resource, and managerial policies, that is another matter. In this latter case, organizations absolutely need to take into account how their core values are or can be meshed with the realities of the global marketplace. Beef is repugnant in a vegetarian country, so what does a hamburger company do? Introduce veggie burgers into its business model. Men dominate business positions in a number of strict, sexually segregated Muslim societies. So what does a Western restaurant chain do that is seeking to operate in those markets? Open separate men's and women's restaurants.

Cultural and legal differences force organizations to accommodate and to adapt, but on occasion organizations do seek to change cultures. Western companies operating in the male-dominated society of Japan realized they were sitting on a gold mine of unused talent in the form of college-educated Japanese women who could not break the glass ceilings of traditional Japanese businesses. After these companies began running circles around their Japanese competitors, some Japanese businesses learned from the Western example and opened doors to women in their own professional ranks. Kellogg's, the breakfast food manufacturer, decided to introduce the concept of eating cereal at breakfast in cultures that were more used to eating sausages or croissants. It has taken a while, but now there is a generation that has come of age in these cultures that regularly pour themselves bowls of cereal for breakfast each morning.

It is possible to change culture, but you need patience and resources, and you must be able to pick and choose your battles wisely. Sometimes cultural practices are there for a reason! Remember the examples introduced in Chapter 2 that demonstrated why some cultural practices should not be changed? One infamous example that Peace Corps volunteers always hear about is the Peace Corps volunteer who set out to change certain hygienic habits in the lesser-developed, rural economy that he was in by introducing the concept of outhouses. He succeeded, but with disastrous consequences. Villages that previously had enjoyed good health became infested with disease due to the poor placement of the outhouses. Think through the possible consequences of your decisions—don't take anything for granted. Nestlé also enjoyed notoriety in the 1970s for introducing and promoting powdered infant formula into lesser-developed countries that had previously relied only on breast-feeding, thus inadvertently introducing contaminated water into infants' diets with fatal consequences.

Nestlé has long since corrected the health problems they helped to create, but their initial experience has been written up in countless international marketing and public relations textbooks as an example of what not to do when operating in a foreign culture. When you operate within your own cultural mind-set in a foreign culture—even with the best intentions—the results can be a lot different from what you intended!

You may or may not try to change cultures in the markets you seek to penetrate abroad. That is not a very helpful statement, is it? No, the real lesson to be learned here is: don't be afraid to think outside the box, but make sure someone familiar with the local culture is part of the planning process who can advise you. Be aware that you are working with potentially explosive materials here!

Sometimes local cultures encourage you to do things that you may not be permitted to do in your own culture. What do you do in these cases such as when "gifts" to decision makers by subcontractors are encouraged or when creating toxic waste dumps is not prohibited? The best rule of thumb in such cases is to refer back to what is legal and ethical in your own country. If you would not do it at home, now is not the time and place to do so—even if it is allowed. Gift giving is considered bribery by the U.S. Department of Commerce and the Justice Department—and they do prosecute U.S. businesses that engage in this in foreign markets under the Foreign Corrupt Practices Act. U.S. lawyers have become very adept at building class action suits for foreign plaintiffs in U.S. courts of law for toxic waste dumps created by U.S. corporate entities. Use the mirror test. If you would blush to be seen doing something at home, then don't do it abroad! The concept of hypocrisy is understood in every culture.

It is not a coincidence that the most advanced and sophisticated markets in the world are the ones exposed to the most outside influences. Differences in thought and culture produce a creative ferment that can generate marvelous new products and ways of doing things that have broad market potential. The best global enterprises are set up to gather information abroad and bring new ideas back for study and possible future use in new product mixes. Globalization is a two-way street, and that is a large part of what makes globalized organizations so interesting and fun to work in—they provide differing perspectives and offer opportunities to compare and contrast. They offer choice and new ways of doing things; apart from their economic impact, it is what makes global organizations such vibrant components of our communities.

Foreign Representatives

Your own language and cultural bias will lead you to those individuals in any market who speak the same language as you do and who can relate to you in your own cultural context. It is useful for you to bear this in mind, as these people may or may not be well regarded in their own circles at home. This is problematic. The best people for you may in fact be people who do not even speak your language and who may have habits and mannerisms that you find "alien." Remember this: the key to your success in any given market is to find the best talent and to ally yourself with the best elements in any given sector—so what do you if the one who approaches you first is not part of this target group? More significantly, how would you even know?

The key to avoiding this problem is the same as always—do your research. These issues that you will be deciding are far too important to leave to chance. Use the resources of the commercial counselor at your local embassy or consulate. Ask your members or stakeholders who they consider to be the local or national leaders in your field. Above all, do not promise anything to anybody until you feel that you have a good understanding of the sector and all the players in that market! Being stuck with an ineffective market representative is a surefire way to costly failure.

This leads to the issue of term limits—a sensitive topic in any culture, but a persistent problem for all membership organizations operating globally.

Term Limits

Those familiar with Washington, D.C., know the very notion of term limits strikes fear into the hearts of all politicians. No politician worth his or her salt wants to give up their hard-earned power without a fight. But, the argument goes, once in power the status quo tends to triumph over change—no matter how badly needed change might be—and the balance of power becomes a little too comfortable for those who have it and uncomfortable for those who don't.

There are two reasons why federally mandated term limits have never gone very far in Washington. The first relates to the constitutional right of voters to elect the representative of their choice. If they want "the same ol' people," then they should be able to have them! The second reason quickly becomes apparent to anyone who comes to Washington as an elected official, and that is, the art of governing is complicated. It takes time to learn the merits of issues and quirks of personalities as well as what works and what doesn't. Until an elected official reaches this level of competence, guess on whom they rely? That's right—the staff! The problem is, who elected the staff?

Virtually all these same issues that roil Washington every few years also are issues for the association community. More than a few associations have boards of directors whose members never seem to change, where new ideas are not welcome, and where newcomers feel as if they are joining a club run by insiders. However, there are many associations with yearlong term limits who push their volunteers through leadership positions so quickly that they hardly have time to make a mark when they are already out the door! We can all think of examples of both types of associations. In the first instance, everything and everybody (including the staff) are run by the board; in the latter, it is the staff that runs the show, with the volunteers happy to be given a brief chance to be in the spotlight.

The overseas chapters of U.S.-based organizations often fall into the first category—their chapter volunteer leaders tend not to change. This is due to a variety of reasons. In those markets where English is a foreign language, the leaders naturally tend to be the ones who are most comfortable with the language, and there may not be many of them to be found. But whether or not language is an issue, in virtually all cases the responsibility of heading the chapter of an international or global organization often conveys a status that is perceived to be valuable and, for this reason, hard to give up.

What is an organization to do? If an organization is weakened by never having any changes in its volunteer leadership, is it weakened if the turnover is too rapid? But where do you draw the line? Good leaders never stay long enough, while poor leaders seem to stay on forever! The key challenge for an association is to offer its membership choice, and this means cultivating future leaders, encouraging them to run for leadership positions, and then stepping aside to allow their membership to select the leader and direction they prefer.

In this time that the World Bank refers to as the "Great Recession," every association needs all the wisdom and flexibility they can find from among their memberships. Democracy, one of the oldest tools in our management toolkit, is perhaps the best way to achieve this.

Flexibility and the Ability to Make Mistakes

Controlling leadership styles and prescriptive, rigid policies can be fatal for international operations that feel uncomfortable with this "foreign way of doing things." If you operate in this fashion or know someone or some organization that does and you think it works, then the chances are great that you are living in a fool's paradise where local operations are observing protocol with a wink and a nod. Worse still is where local operations are performing exactly as they are supposed to but with lackluster results.

Introducing changes in customs in a foreign culture can be risky. It can either be a total flop or it can produce marvelous results. What works in one culture does not necessarily produce the same positive results in another.

A longtime member of the European Union, Spain is finding that its three-hour lunch period that allows for its famous midday siesta is slowly disappearing because Spanish offices find it increasingly inconvenient in dealing with pressing business matters that come to them midday from non-siesta countries! Exposed to the global ebb and flow of business, Spain is coming to its own conclusions about the need to "go along to get along," and as a result it is finding its three-hour midday siesta shrinking slowly to naught. Forcing this change artificially through corporate mandates would probably not have worked quite so well.

As an American manager in Brussels with a host of European employees from multiple countries, I found it curious that the Europeans insisted on having offices with doors that they would close behind them each day while "the American" kept his door wide open in a friendly, American-style "open door policy." The example didn't catch on and the Europeans asserted their space and kept their doors closed. But was this really an important issue? Not really. What is important is to choose your battles wisely—some cultural issues may be worth the fight, while others clearly are not. Be flexible.

Empowering employees by taking away their fear of punishment if they fail in an honest effort is a management technique that is widely regarded as useful in many cultures. It is particularly useful when operating in a foreign environment where cultural differences almost guarantee there will be different ways of doing things. The important thing is for everyone to understand and to take into account what the organization's strategic goals and intermediate objectives are that must be realized—then let them find the best way to achieve them. You might be surprised at the creativity you have unleashed. There has been more than one occasion where global organizations have repatriated ways of doing things that are an improvement over the traditions and processes in their headquarters. As stated in the famous Alka-Seltzer commercial: "Try it, you'll like it!" Instill in your organization the ability to accept failure but also to learn from it. Remember, madness is trying the same thing over and over but expecting different results!

How flexible should you be in this global potpourri of cultural differences? As the question implies, every organization has values that cross cultural boundaries and on which no compromise is possible. As your organization grows globally, it becomes even more important to know and to affirm what those strategic values are. Indeed, what are "strategic values"?

Being True to Your Word

When you travel or operate abroad in any manner, you may or may not be aware that there are a thousand eyes on you. You are most certainly being observed—you are a foreigner. You stand out. As such, you are being measured for the respect you show your host country as well as the nature of your own character. What do you stand for? Do your actions demonstrate that you are true to anything greater than your own self-interest? If the answer is affirmative to this last question, you are in a better position than not—even if your set of beliefs is different from your host country. Hypocrisy is a universally despised character flaw.

Cross-cultural exposure leads us to ask fundamental questions of ourselves, which can sometimes be helpful to aspiring global managers. On this point, a local business school here in Washington, D.C., is running an advertisement with the following question as a lead: *What's the word on the street about your word?* Catchy, isn't it? It makes you stop and ask yourself, "Am I seen to be as good as my word?" Whatever your answer, why is this question even important? As we all know, all's fair in love and war and business . . . or is it?

I would argue that a leader who is perceived to be as good as his word and as someone who is reliable and true has a built-in advantage over someone who is not. The leader who inspires trust has business partners and colleagues and friends who will go the extra distance for him—the others not.

In this low-context culture that we live in, in the United States and Canada and most of western Europe, we do not need to know another person very well to do business with them. All we have to do is negotiate the broad terms of a deal, have the lawyers draw up the contract, and then we are in business! But most of the rest of the world are high-context cultures. They do not do business with people they do not know well; and contracts—if they exist at all—are usually a minor formality, because the dishonor associated with failing to deliver on a promise carries far more shame than a broken contract.

Could it be that a problem with our low-context culture is that we can too easily delegate our commitments to be handled by lawyers, brokers, and assorted go-betweens and that in the process we risk losing that aspect of our soul that characterizes true leaders in all cultures? In the ruinous economy of 2008–2010, which is the direct result of too many cavalier attitudes toward personal responsibility, maybe this is a point worthy of all our reflection.

When in Rome

The key to success in this global economy that we are living in is in being able to identify those ideas or concepts that have universal potential and then to adapt them to local need and conditions. It is on this last point that many organizations fail. Language and cultural differences are not inconsequential. The marketers at Chevrolet realized this after they famously introduced their best-selling car called the "Chevy Nova" into Spanish-speaking markets. The Spanish phrase *no-va* means "does not go or does not work"—which the Chevrolet marketers learned quickly, to their everlasting embarrassment!

To successfully meet these challenges, your organization needs to blend into each market as if it belonged there. In fact, that is the principal challenge—to show that you do belong there! This requires doing your homework thoroughly ahead of time as well as being fortunate enough to tap into the kind and quality of local talent that you will need to guide you through all the potential cultural pitfalls and beyond, to success.

The Tug of War between Local and Global

Humans are both rational and emotional beings. Our emotional side likes what is familiar and that which makes us feel special. Icelanders take pride in their eye-watering national dish *hakarl* (rotten shark that has reached is fermented state after having been buried for a while) that only Icelanders can appreciate! But our rational side is more practical. We make choices on what is most convenient, cheaper, faster, and more efficient. And we make decisions based on what conveys the most status.

These tendencies pull us in two opposite directions. On the one hand, we cherish our differences, but on the other hand, we like and seek to be as efficient, modern, and status-conscious and anyone—including people around the world from us. One appeals to our instincts to be rooted at the local level, while the other pulls us toward globalization.

These tendencies are manifesting themselves in measurable ways. On the one hand, we have more independent countries existing in the world today that at any time in human history. Globalization has made the expression of individuality more possible now than at any time in the past. Nations exist today such as Ukraine and the

Czech Republic and many others that have not existed in a thousand years—if ever! On the other hand, every year that goes by witnesses the disappearance of more living languages. There are fewer and fewer languages spoken today than were spoken a decade ago, and there will be fewer still in the decade to come. And this, too, is a direct consequence of globalization.

Once while visiting Brittany, a historic Celtic region of France, I remarked to the French lady who was accompanying me how sad it was to see the Breton language and colorful folkloric costumes of Brittany disappear with the passing of generations. She responded, "But how are you going to convince a teenage Breton girl that she should dress the old-fashioned way while the girls of Paris are dressing in the latest fashions?" How, indeed?

Cultures and languages are not made to be put into museums. They are made to serve very practical purposes, and once they cease to fill this function, they do pass into history. This is the nature of any evolution—human or otherwise. So, too, the globalization strategies and tactics of organizations—to have any assurance of longevity, your organization needs to hone in on what is most practical, that which helps people to grow personally and professionally in the most cost-effective and efficient ways possible.

Every survey of international membership organizations shows the same thing—members most closely relate to the local contacts they have with the organization, less with the national presence, and still less with the international headquarters. People tend to relate best and be loyal to that which is closest to them and which they see on a regular basis. National and international headquarters will always be "out of sight, out of mind." Your success in global expansion is in recognizing and accommodating yourself to this fact, even while striving to identify universal solutions to common local problems or needs.

The most successful global organizations are those that operate profitably and effectively at the local level but that also continually identify, package, and deliver the kinds of products and services that are needed by the global economy in a timely, cost-effective manner. Global organizations thrive when people and companies at the local level identify with them and welcome them into their lives and businesses. The old Vaudeville comedians had a well-known line that always brought laughs because people knew what was meant: "That's no lady, that's my wife!" The loyal customers/members/stakeholders of global organizations might offer a similar line—"That's no global organization, that's my (substitute here what you want—such as favorite place of business, professional organization, place that I most relate to . . .)." People relate to organizations on a micro or local basis, but for these operations to enjoy long-term sustainability they must be relevant to the trends and market needs that manifest themselves at the macro or global level; although people like the near and the familiar, they also recognize that in the long term they need to follow the paths that ensure survival and growth.

For a global organization to have a great idea but be unable to apply it locally is not very useful—in fact, it may as well have no idea at all. But focusing uniquely at the local level without connecting the dots, without trying to derive solutions to universal problems and needs at a global level is also an organizational dead-end. Scales need weights on both ends in order to be in balance.

The organizational challenge here, then, is to be able to function fluently and effectively at both levels—to be able to make global solutions relevant at the local level where people live, as well as to be able to derive lessons from what is learned locally in order to apply these concepts globally. Moreover, getting it right once doesn't mean you can rest on your laurels. Global tides and local currents are constantly changing, leading to the never-ending need for global organizations to be in a constant mode of seeking out areas where they can improve their effectiveness, efficiency, and relevancy on both the global and local levels. How's that for a challenge? Who said globalization was easy?

Chapter 6

Endeavors in Specific Countries

Those associations that performed the best during the Great Recession of 2008–2010 were those that served the broadest and most diverse base of markets—so that the decline in some markets was compensated by stronger performance in other markets. In particular, those associations that had a presence in the fast-growing markets of China and India outperformed those whose presence was confined to the United States or Europe. This chapter discusses successful strategies in penetrating the two fastest-growing markets of the world—China and India—as well as techniques by which associations have cataloged and prioritized opportunities in markets elsewhere in the world.

Global Strategies Begin with Research

Research is critical in developing successful global strategies. Why? Simply because (1) implementation of global strategies is expensive, and (2) implementation takes a number of years to be successful. Too many associations march off to invest in or set up operations in declining markets or invest wrongly in growing markets. They would have done better to have stayed at home! Among the key research is (1) whether the association has goods and services of value to those outside the United States, (2) whether there is any verified demand for these goods and services, and (3) the expense of sales and distribution versus the added revenues. Association membership has the same challenges to research as goods and services, that is, whether there is any value in membership to non-U.S. members, whether there is any demand for membership from outside the United States, and the cost of membership services versus the added dues revenues. Membership expansion can be more difficult to research than goods and services for many reasons. For example, many associations don't know what their cost to service new and renewing U.S. members is annually. And who knows what a new member in an emerging market nation expects in the way of value, and what that member can afford to pay in annual dues?

One struggling U.S.-based, automobile-centered trade association took note that associations operating internationally were doing better than those like themselves that were only domestically centered. In the pressing situation they found themselves in, they did not feel they had the time, expertise, or money to invest in doing any research—but this didn't stop them from investing in projects to develop their presence in Europe, where the automobile market was in even greater decline. Personal familiarity with certain markets—which was the basis for this association's decision—is certainly useful, but only if those are the right markets to be in relative to all the other opportunities. The world is a big place—so big that no organization is big enough or rich enough to make the wrong decisions when it comes to global market development strategies. Organizations do drop tons of money into unproductive markets and never hear it hit bottom. Such mistakes can be fatal to an organization—not only because of the time and financial resources lost, but also because of loss of credibility within its own constituent base that might quite rightly wonder how this wasteful use of their hard-earned resources benefits them. Making the right decision starts with good research.

So where are the opportunities in this global picture? It depends on what sector you are in, but the macroeconomic trends are pretty clear.

We are in the midst of revolutionary changes in the world's economic balance of power.

If you rank the 190 national markets of the world by gross domestic product (GDP) today, you get a picture that is vaguely similar to the traditional picture of the economies that have dominated the world since before the First World War. But if you throw in economic and population growth trends as a factor in your calculations, this picture changes quite dramatically. In this picture, China and India start to assume an importance that grows only if you project these figures forward another 10 or 15 years. By the time the current generation has reached retirement age and a new generation has assumed control, the world will be almost unrecognizable. The U.S. economy will still be large, but it will no longer be the largest, and Europe will almost have disappeared from the picture as an economically dominant region. Although Europe still factors as an important player for reasons described later, the Atlantic-centered dominance of the world economy is disappearing.

China and India are two of the largest markets in the world, and their importance is only going to increase. In 2007, India's GDP was US$1,176.89 billion and growing at a rate of between 9 and 10 percent annually. Meanwhile, China had a GDP of US$3,205.51 billion in 2007, growing at a staggering rate of 13 percent annually. Together, the two countries represent over a third of the world's population, and as the countries develop they will have an even greater influence on the world stage than they do today.

Opportunities and threats are often the opposite sides of the same coin. Today, these two big emerging markets (BEMs) represent huge opportunities for Western standards-making and professional development organizations. But as these countries emerge into their own with the standards and training programs that they have come to use, it will inevitably cause others to question the relevancy of those organizations that have not played a role there.

Entering the Chinese Market

There is no nation or business entity in the world today that is not directly or indirectly affected by China. China's government estimates its population at somewhere between 1.3 and 1.6 billion persons—note that the margin of error is as large as the entire population of the United States, or most of the European Union!

Poised in 2010 to pass Japan as the world's second-largest economy, China's average annual growth rate in the manufacturing sector has been in excess of 14 percent, and its annual growth rate in the services sector has been in excess of 8 percent—growth rates that are second only to India. During the past 10 to 15 years when new construction was centered in and around Shanghai, it was estimated that Shanghai accounted for more than 50 percent of the total number of construction cranes that were in use in the world. China is a market that is so hungry for growth that it is virtually sucking up the world's financial and material resources. And its Confucian-rooted culture places a premium on hard work, self-improvement, and learning—characteristics that ensure that every professional certification, training, and educational program that is offered in that country is oversubscribed.

Isn't this market ideally suited to the roles typically played by trade associations and professional societies? Indeed so. If yours is a membership-based association, you have undoubtedly seen growing membership interest over the past few years from China, and your leadership probably is developing a strategy for better serving this market or is puzzling about how to do so.

In this case, it is prudent to "puzzle" because for all the incredible opportunities China represents, no one who is familiar with China would characterize it as an easy market to penetrate. This is particularly true of associations that do not have any sort of sanctioned legal status in China—but more on that later.

Traditionally, there are four ways of working with or in China:

- The first, which is the least expensive and least risky, is to export your products or services there—in other words, to serve the market from a distance. The advantage of this arrangement is the relative lack of risk while the disadvantage is that you are handicapped in being able to grow and expand into all the opportunities that China offers.
- The second is to take advantage of China's relatively new franchising laws to develop an in-country presence by licensing or franchising arrangements. The Chinese government officially

encourages this mode of entry, and any visitor to China cannot help but notice the enormous success of virtually every franchise you can think of—they are all there.

- The third is through equity or joint ventures—a risky arrangement that used to be the only method of foreign investment sanctioned by the government. It is risky because if the joint venture fails, there is little the foreign owner can do to prevent its assets—including intellectual property—from later being used by its former Chinese partners.
- The fourth is through wholly owned foreign enterprises (WOFEs—pronounced "woofies") through which the foreign investor sets up its own government-recognized presence in China. The advantage of this approach is that you have total control over your operations in China, but the disadvantage is that you have to make a relatively important investment of capital and time to get started—and unless you have done a thorough job of researching the market and found just the right people to staff your operation, you could lose a significant amount of money and time before your investments pay off—if they ever do.

These four modes of market entry are not mutually exclusive. Many foreign investors can and do use a combination of approaches to crack this fascinating market.

But as noted, associations have a special problem. Communist governments (even former Communist governments, as can be seen through recent developments in Russia where the government summarily closed down all nongovernmental organizations [NGOs] operating in that country) are particularly interested in controlling any and all membership organizations—especially organizations that offer education and training programs. For this reason, the only official associations in China are those that are quasi-governmental.

Literature—both hard copy and digital versions transmitted through the Internet—that is imported into China is closely examined and sometimes blocked. Membership fees in organizations that are not officially recognized are difficult to collect—particularly if funds have to be transmitted outside the country. And, technically, any unofficial gathering of more than a handful of people anywhere in China is against the law. This situation presents an interesting dilemma for Western hemisphere membership-based associations.

Those few associations that do have a presence in China do so through "rep" offices. These are offices that promote the association and its programs, but which do not collect dues or officially organize membership meetings.

Official recognition of associations could take many years. In the interim, Western associations need to be innovative, and they need to have recourse to the single most important factor for success in China: *guanxi* (pronounced gwan-chee), which, roughly translated, means "connections" or "relationships." China is a culture of relationships. In marketing terminology, China would be referred to as a high-context culture—as opposed to our American low-context culture that allows us to do business with strangers fairly easily. The Chinese typically do not casually enter into business arrangements. Foreign entities need to choose a Chinese partner that has guanxi—the relationships needed to help launch your endeavor successfully. Bear in mind that there is good guanxi and bad guanxi. Good in this case means knowing the right people to make a business venture work, while bad refers to graft and corruption—which is a problem in China and to be avoided at all cost.

Apart from these cultural considerations, local contacts are crucial because of China's sometimes overbearing bureaucracy and because of the many languages spoken throughout the country.

Have all of these considerations frightened you yet? They should! But turning away from a market this big and growing this fast is not an option. China does not offer easy success, but it does represent tremendous opportunity to those with flexibility, intelligence, hard work, and persistence—all qualities highly valued in China.

Succeeding in India

As of 2009, India was the 10th largest economy, fourth in terms of purchasing power with growth between 9 and 10 percent. Its GDP is estimated to be $719.8 billion. Since becoming an open economy in 1991, India has worked to make its mark in the global market. With the average age of its citizens at 27 years, many of whom are well educated, married, and without children, India has the ability and resources to be among the top four nations in terms of economy. The following are 10 lessons to follow when beginning business operations in India.

Many companies enter India thinking they know how to be successful. They may have a successful global brand and believe that the name alone will ensure success. The first lesson for succeeding in India is to assume that you know very little. Making a bad assumption on a target market, business function, or the necessities of a population is 100 times worse than ignorance. This arrogance and authoritative nature will get you nowhere.

Past travel in a country, a taste for the local cuisine, or a family friend that is from the area does not mean that you know about the culture and business practices of a nation. Learn about the cultural differences and adjust your business style and marketing strategy accordingly. These simple actions will place you one step closer to success.

The second lesson for succeeding in India is to set up your own structure. In India, a company-owned structure outperforms third-party distribution by a factor of four to seven. Businesses that have their own "eyes and ears on the ground" tend to be more successful and adaptive to the home site and the local site. The failure rate of a joint venture exceeds 90 percent. Given this fact, lesson three is no joint ventures. Over three to five years, a 100 percent subsidiary will outperform any joint venture.

Lesson four relates to acquisitions and does not necessarily apply to associations, but is a good guideline to follow. An acquisition strategy is only as good as the target available. The majority of acquisitions are overpriced and end up as a can of worms. Therefore, be prepared to walk away.

Lesson five covers one of the most important resources needed, money. Whether your organization makes a loss or a profit during the first couple of years, you will need larger amounts of cash in subsequent years. This lesson advises to plan for this element.

Lesson six relates to corporate and product branding. This is often the most effective source of competitive advantage in the Indian marketplace. And in this regard, public relations and word-of-mouth marketing in this marketplace is more effective than a classic advertising campaign.

Finding a person to be head of the new operation is often the most difficult decision you will face. The life and death of an organization lies with this person. The person best fit for this role has execution and operations experience and isn't necessarily an expert on strategy. Lesson seven is finding an individual with the characteristics necessary to be successful. You want to find an individual who has "hands-on competent leadership." The most effective at this position are the ignored hungry souls at the second or third rung who have the desire and competitive spirit to succeed in a foreign environment.

Lesson eight for succeeding in India is centered on innovation. Develop a business model that incorporates innovation and market adaptations. It is necessary to adapt the product or service to the local market. Know the cultural differences and adapt a concept for the new market. The supply chain will need to be altered in order to accommodate this new market.

This idea of innovation is captured with the term *LOGAN*, which stands for localized global innovation. Logan is also a new model of Renault car that was specifically created for a local target market and is now being distributed in other markets. This car shows how Renault adjusted its model to fit the needs of the market.

Lesson nine is an important link to global operations. You can capture value for your organization by linking your business in India to your global operations. Create a hub for global research and development and make India a source of components and materials. The resources needed are available to make it a center for information technology (IT) development and support as well as a service center for human resources (HR) and finance.

The main idea derived from this lesson is to leverage the advantage, make use of the resources and opportunities that have been made available to you.

The final lesson for succeeding in India is that in order to capture India's full potential, the branch must report to the world headquarters, not the Asia structure. The operations in India should be positioned within the whole organization.

Special Challenges in Transatlantic Relations

A U.S.-based association in struggling to overcome problems associated with its growing international membership on either side of the Atlantic discovered that its problems were complicated, far reaching, and also virtually identical to the problems faced by many other associations.

If you are the executive of an international association or an association with a growing membership base on either side of the Atlantic, you may find it reassuring to know your problems are not unique and in fact probably not even of your making. What are these problems, where do they come from, and what can be done about them?

Let's call this "association X." Association X is a trade association representing a rapidly growing sector of the professional services industry. As is the case with many trade associations, association X became international through the expanding international operations of its members.

However, many of the overseas operations of their member companies were separate legal entities. While they shared names and had certain other arrangements with their U.S. counterparts, they otherwise were autonomous. Because of this, they felt they needed to have a separate presence in the association. Little by little, the involvement of these overseas affiliates drew other companies from their markets into the membership ranks of what had been a primarily U.S.-dominated trade association. Almost before they knew it, one half of the association's members were from outside the United States.

Problems began surfacing almost immediately. The Europeans, recognizing the force of their numbers, demanded an equal presence on the board and the transformation of a U.S.-oriented association into one that was more international, if not global in outlook and structure. The Americans welcomed making a place at the table for their European counterparts, but there were a couple of fundamental problems that needed to be addressed.

The first was that the Europeans were not paying as much as the Americans in supporting the international association. The Europeans did not deny this but pointed out that their national and regional structure created two levels of activity and management that needed to be funded, whereas the Americans had only one. When taking all this into account the Europeans noted that they were paying as much if not more than the Americans for activities that were just as valuable to the association as what the Americans were doing. The feeling of the Americans was straightforward, if not very understanding—if the Europeans wanted to participate in the association they should pay their fair share for international activities.

The second problem related to the nature of the relationship of the American multinationals with their own European affiliates. The Americans saw them as an extension of their U.S.-headquartered corporate operations, but the Europeans did not see themselves in the same way. When it came to deciding matters relating to professional standards, dues payments, and other professional priorities, the European affiliates felt more at ease siding with their European competitors than with their American colleagues.

As they tried to devise solutions to these problems there were many times when it looked like the association was simply going to fall apart. At first we thought these problems stemmed from the peculiarities of the personalities involved. But as we have worked with other associations in the fields of health care, manufacturing, accounting, and auditing, and others we have seen a repetition of the same problems and frustrations.

The problem begins with unrealistic expectations. We have heard so much about the global economy that we risk minimizing the very real linguistic, cultural, legislative, and regulatory differences that exist between countries. Charles de Gaulle called America "the daughter of Europe." Indeed, America is largely an offshoot of Europe, but we who live here know just how diverse and different we are compared to Europe. However, that does not stop us from jumping to our own erroneous conclusion that there are no problems or differences that cannot be managed. We are surprised and possibly slightly wounded when we learn that the Europeans like—even cherish—their differences. They do not want to be made into Americans, even for the sake of greater efficiency!

Taken as a whole, Europe is the most economically powerful region of the world, yet the United States continues to define cutting-edge thinking and research in most areas of professional activity. If you are part of an association, it is inevitable that you, too, will find yourself embroiled in your own transatlantic tug-of-war over issues of governance, standards, and sharing of resources. There is no way to avoid it.

Here are some lessons learned:

- Develop a vision for your association. Among other issues, determine if you wish to be international or multinational, and make sure your members know the difference.

- Recognize and accept the basic differences that exist between the national markets of your members and identify what you have in common.
- If you are seeing that your regular national members are reluctant to see their dues increase, know that this is even more the case for an international organization. Resist the temptation to build a mini-UN. Keep overhead to a minimum and link payments to products and services. Your members need to know what they are getting for their money, and it needs to be something tangible. Recognize and communicate the effects of (1) the diverse earning power of individuals in various countries and (2) the effect of diverse national currency valuations and currency exchanges to and from U.S. dollars.
- Finally, learn to see that diversity is good and that the road to a global economy is hard. If you steel yourself and your members to expect difficulty and differences of opinion, then you may be less discouraged when you actually encounter them!

When compared to the growth trends of such markets as China and India, Europe's significance as a market opportunity is diminishing, but its presence as a challenge to the United States' traditional dominance in the area of standards and certification is growing.

The many countries that became the European Union (EU) went through an arduous process spanning more than 20 years to harmonize their various product and professional standards into one European standard. This relatively fresh experience has given them a certain credibility when they assert on the world stage that they alone know how to develop global standards and that the European standards in and of themselves are more global than other standards—particularly U.S. standards—that are more focused on the needs and perspectives of just one country. This is the perspective that the International Organization for Standardization (ISO) and many European nations like to distribute, enabling them to position themselves as the "true" global standards-setting body. Actually, many U.S. standards-setting bodies develop global standards through a global participation process. The key is the extent to which there is a commitment to global participation in the process, not whose logo is on the letterhead. Savvy U.S.-based standards-setting organizations have known and practiced this for years.)

U.S.-European relations have always contained slightly more rivalry than cooperation—none more so than now, as shown in the area of global standards.

Following the Flag

Alphabetical listings of associations in the United States always have their largest number of names in the "A" column—partly because many start with the word *association*, but also because many names start with the descriptive word *American*. Is this a help or a handicap when operating in markets outside the United States?

The easy answer to this question is: "It depends!"

The United States remains one of the world's largest and most open markets for imports of goods and services, as well as imported labor and professional skills. So, to the extent that a person or an organization is focused on penetrating the U.S. market, belonging to or being certified or accredited through a U.S. association that is clearly labeled as such is a clear advantage. And, for this reason, there are numerous instances of American-labeled nonprofits that each year successfully attract hundreds of members and customers from outside the United States.

Problems start when the U.S. members of such organizations start to become sanguine in the belief that their products and services are superior to any other that can be found anywhere in the world—because this is less and less the case.

There are two factors at play here.

First, success breeds competition. In almost every economic sector, nonprofits based outside the United States are challenging U.S. credentials by offering more "international" credentials of their own. Many, if not most, of the competition is coming from the countries of the EU, who believe they invented the concept.

There is some truth to this claim. Since 1986, when the "Single Act" was first signed that led to the creation of the EU, the European countries have been working overtime to harmonize their individual national standards from professional and academic credentials to product and organizational standards. The EU now comprises 25 countries, and they rightfully feel they are experts in international standards harmonization. If you have not noticed it yet, these European standards are being marketed around the world as the only true "international" option. In moments of candor, these European competitors have been known to be critical of American standards as representing a U.S.-centric "do it my way" approach.

Such European rivalry, once no more annoying than a small mosquito, has now emerged as a very serious competitor—ignored only by the most benighted. The Europeans have been effective in taking their message and products to the global market because of the increasing attractiveness of their own market—the EU is now the largest economy in the world. And the EU has also become increasingly attractive, as the image and standing of the United States has declined in markets and cultures around the globe.

Second, the U.S. economic dominance in the world market is declining rapidly. Without debating the reasons for this phenomenon, no one can deny that relative to the rest of the world, and although still large, the U.S. economy is shrinking. This fact dramatically undercuts the perceived value of the American brand.

The wild cards in this changing world scenario are India and China, who, for the time being, are playing to both the European and American leads simultaneously (why not?). But it is interesting to note that in certain critical technologies China is busy developing its own standards. Given China's phenomenal growth, our children's generation could well be marching to the beat of a Chinese drummer later in this century.

Given these facts, what is an American-labeled association to do?

First, don't cede the global market to anybody—go global yourself! The models have been well established now by others. Find the approach that fits your organization's goals and success measures the best and implement it. Remember, though, going global is not the same as operating internationally. You know you are global when members cannot honestly say what the nationality of the organization is—in other words, your association has taken root in everyone's native soil.

As a part of going global, take an unbiased look at your organization's name. Organizations that have determined that a global path is their future have either changed their name to an acronym that reflects the organization's origins at the same time as its global mission and is pronounceable and useable in any language or culture, or they have restructured themselves to create a global organization in structure and name that becomes the delivery mechanism through which your organization expands.

The United States started as a nation of shrewd traders who knew their markets and what each needed. At this point in our global economy, those markets need global organizations and global credentials that have local relevance. Respond to this need and your organization will grow. Ignore it and you risk losing relevance yourself!

Relative Merits of These Markets

As China and India face off to determine which country will dominate the 21st century and beyond, we are going to see a growing rivalry that hopefully will not extend past the peaceful economic kind. There clearly is much at stake, and the leaders of both nations realize this all too well. But there is no reason why those of us who are from outside these two countries should feel the need to take sides—both demand our attention. We discussed the strengths of both markets earlier, but following are some areas to watch.

Other Considerations and Concerns

China. China is the largest, fastest-growing economy on earth and is likely to remain so for some time.

As a centralized economy, China can make virtually anything happen it wants to see happen. Were people attending the Olympic Games worried about the pollution in Beijing? No problem! The government closed down all smoke-emitting factories and traffic a few months before the games to clear the air. Does the old Shanghai have the potential to resume its glory as a sophisticated city as well as trading center? No problem! The government issued requests for proposals from the world's leading architectural firms to design the dazzling bouquets of skyscrapers that now distinguish Shanghai's skyline. And what happened to the old, run-down parts of the city where these skyscrapers were placed? No problem! Entire sections of the city were razed and their populations relocated. If you are on the good side of China's government, you do not have to worry about red tape or lack of resources of any kind. Life has never been so easy!

However, suppose you are not on the government's radar screen? Then life can be difficult. You will need help getting attention and getting approvals and protecting your intellectual property. This is a market with a lot of sharp elbows, so you will need well-placed connections, constant diligence, and a lot of hard work to break in!

One can never forget that China has a Communist government. Not only is power centralized, but so is thinking. There is literally one party line for virtually any subject, which leads people to be very cautious before expressing their opinion about any policy matter, however trivial. Organizational membership in anything other than Communist party organizations is not recognized. Meetings of more than a few people at a time need to be submitted ahead of time for approval. And distribution of written information of any kind is highly regulated.

Westerners can and do adapt to these facts of life pretty easily in present-day China. But the Chinese themselves are not so comfortable. As the educated Chinese middle class increases, it is clear that they are increasingly restive about the intellectual and ideological straitjacket they find themselves in when compared to those they know in most other countries. Periodically, the government cracks down hard and very publicly on overt symbols of political resistance; but how much longer can this continue before it causes wider instability domestically or even internationally? When pressed, centralized governments often try to maintain control over their own people by finding or provoking crises outside their country. Outside threats have a way of galvanizing a population unified by patriotic fervor, although it is hard to keep such nationalistic feelings revved up for long without causing serious trouble with your neighbors and the world at large!

At some point it is certain that either China will become more democratic or its growing internal pressures will cause it to implode. Lacking any sort of democratic model in its past, such turmoil might only serve to replace one form of totalitarian rule with another. And if such a thing were to happen, the turmoil and uncertainty that this would create for investors and trading partners would be considerable. It is something to be aware of. It is China's one serious weak spot.

Demographically, China's one-child policy also promises to create certain economic and social strains as their population ages and is replaced by a smaller generation who will be responsible not only for building the economy but also for supporting the huge generation represented by their retired parents.

India. As anyone from the United States and the United Kingdom knows who has ever called a customer help or reservation center and ended up in Mumbai—India's official language is English. It is, in fact, the largest English-using country in the world—a fact that makes it very attractive to any and all organizations that seek to sell materials and training courses in English, or that run corporate call centers! Furthermore, unlike China, India has an independent judiciary, and it is the largest democracy in the world—institutions and traditions that should serve India well as it copes with the pains and challenges associated with rapid and prolonged economic growth. Most of these are good things, right?

Unfortunately, this is not all. India is also the home of famously rigid, slow-moving, and not very helpful bureaucracies. It takes forever to get approvals for anything—a fact that has led to major problems with graft and corruption. Although India has a very impressive educated elite and a burgeoning middle class, these facts are sometimes overshadowed by the country's tremendous poverty and illiteracy, as well as the social prejudices stemming from its ancient caste system. Like China, India is incredibly thirsty for Western investment and know-how, but the sensitivities associated with a colonial past simultaneously can make for a certain suspicion of foreign presence of any kind. On this last point, China and India are in accord; the bottom line for the governments in both countries is: foreign economic involvement of any kind needs to benefit China and India, or it is not welcome.

Gender equality is still distant in India. Although in modern times India has had a woman as a national leader and China has not, women are much more in evidence in positions of power in both the private and public sectors in China than is the case in India. On the street level, Western women traveling in the two countries usually prefer China, where they feel they receive more egalitarian treatment and are less exposed to sexual harassment than is typically the case in India. As a rule, Indian families tend to spend less time and money educating their daughters than their sons, which leads to a tremendous waste of human resources. This is a strategic weakness for India that could be turned into an opportunity for Western organizations operating in that market who may be interested in tapping into this eager and available supply of talent.

Other "Low-Hanging Fruit" in Global Markets

Because of their large size (and for China and India, their record-breaking growth), China and India, followed by Europe, are the usual points of focus for organizations seeking to expand globally. But other geo-economic, geopolitical, and cultural considerations also offer appeal.

Other BEMs. Big emerging markets, or BEMs, are defined as large, fast-growing, developing economies that dominate the economies of a particular geographic region. These economies suck up resources of all kinds and typically produce strong returns on investment. China and India are clearly the BEMs of Asia and due to their sustained, extraordinary growth are poised in the coming decade to become the globe's primary economic drivers. As regional powers, Brazil and Mexico play this role for Latin America. Africa's BEM is South Africa. And Europe's BEM is Russia—leading economists to refer to the BRIC countries that are driving global growth: Brazil, Russia, India, and China. In terms of going where the money is or where the growth is, it makes sense for associations to give these markets primary consideration.

The "Anglo-Saxon Mafia"—Australia, Canada, New Zealand, the United Kingdom, and the United States

With the exception of Canada's French language policy, all these countries share approximately the same level of economic development, the same cultural heritage, and of course the same language. All of these factors make it easy and relatively cost-efficient for associations to expand their programs and memberships into these international markets. While organizations based in France tend to gravitate to those markets around the world that are former French colonies and that continue to rely on French law, customs, and language, so, too, can those organizations that use English as their language of business look to English-speaking countries as offering friendly grounds for expansion. These markets may not be the largest or fastest-growing, but their cultural similarities make them easier to penetrate for organizations that operate within that same culture.

Emerging and Lesser-Developed Markets

These are markets that have been identified for geopolitical and economic reasons by national and multilateral grant-making and lending agencies to be eligible to receive various kinds of financial and development aid. Sometimes this aid takes the form of loans from the International Monetary Fund (IMF) or major national governments (such as the U.S. Department of the Treasury) to help bolster a country's embattled currency. Sometimes the aid is in the form of World Bank or bilateral development agency (such as the U.S. Agency for International Development [USAID], to which most of the world's developed countries have a counterpart) grants or loans for infrastructure development and projects to promote the transfer of critical professional skills and standards that will help increase a developing country's prospects for sustainable growth.

It is this last point that offers opportunities to nonprofit organizations that are responsible for product or professional standards or that can develop and run training programs that are designed to help people and organizations reach these standards.

When these international development programs first started, shortly after the end of the Second World War, a lot of their work was in constructing roads, bridges, power plants, schools, and dams. But it did not take too long to realize that true improvements in a country's economic outlook could be achieved only by investing in its people. The reasoning goes that if a developing country's civil and agricultural engineers, health care workers, schoolteachers, and business leaders are trained to the levels and in the best practices of the world's leading economies, then the country's economic future should take care of itself.

Corruption has been a major impediment to growth in much of the developing world. In helping to address this problem, one U.S.-based professional society, the Institute of Internal Auditors (IIA), has been a valued participant in World Bank and USAID programs. Internal auditing consists of the professional discipline of designing and administering programs internal to an organization that will help proof it against improper use of the organization's resources. The IIA was established nearly 100 years ago to serve the needs of the professionals operating in this area. Among other services, the IIA has a certification arm that tests and certifies that internal auditors have met the minimum standards of the profession. The IIA also provides classes to help people just entering this profession.

Developing this match-up with World Bank and USAID programs has served all entities well. Through the IIA, development agencies have been able to disseminate programs that have been proven to help reduce corruption in emerging market countries, while the IIA itself has been able to offer its members short overseas assignments for these teaching missions on an all-expenses-paid basis that have generated revenue for their organization while creating goodwill for the IIA in new markets abroad. In fact, wherever the IIA has operated such programs, they have succeeded in leaving behind overseas chapters full of new IIA members! For the IIA this is a classic case of doing well by doing good.

Identifying Markets Abroad that Are Best for Your Organization

Trade associations, professional societies, and other individual membership organizations should keep track of the markets where their members have a presence. You might be surprised at the patterns you discover and the opportunities they present for expansion abroad. One U.S.-based engineering society, before it had developed a formal international program, had known that they had members with overseas mailing addresses, but they had not kept track of this in any systematic way. When they did project these membership locations on a map, they saw that there were membership groupings in Nigeria, Saudi Arabia, and Venezuela, but they had not made the connection until then that the petroleum industry could be an important conduit for building their overseas presence.

For associations, like any other private-sector organization, expansion into overseas markets is or should be entirely about business opportunity. BEMs are logical places to begin to look for opportunities, but everything depends on the characteristics of markets that will be best for you.

There is a three-step process for identifying the markets abroad that are best for your organization.

1. Start by analyzing where your current overseas members, customers, or stakeholders come from, if you have any. Like the engineering association just described, you may discover a natural pattern that can point the way forward for developing your globalization strategy.
2. If you do not currently have any overseas contacts, then examine your domestic members and stakeholders to see where their overseas interests might be.
3. Develop a profile of your domestic base in a way that defines the types of overseas markets that will be of most interest.

Once you have developed a list of possible markets abroad, then you will need to investigate further the strategic environment that is offered in each for your organization. Your "strategic environment" is reflected in a classical SWOT analysis: the *strengths* you have to build on for that particular market; the *weaknesses* you may have to address; the *opportunities* that might be there to build on existing or new relationships or funding programs; and the *threats* that might exist from competitors, and legal and cultural barriers.

Analyzing World Markets— Tailor-Making Your Approach

Table 6.1 is a grid that was easily and quickly developed for one association that runs education and training programs to compare and contrast the opportunities they have in various global markets. Note how they drew on internal resources such as their board members and other clients and stakeholders for information and integrated this with market facts that are readily available through secondary sources of research.

Table 6.1 Analysis of World Markets

Region/ Country	Total Potential as a Target Audience (Based on population, age, wealth, size)	Competition/ Allies	Current Association Presence	Potential Sponsorship	Other Considerations
Taiwan	√	Not much	Some courses	Has been some in past	Big emerging market; professionals love a credential and education self-improvement, go beyond a rep office—need to get official recognition; everything works by relationship
China	√	Not much	Some course interest expressed	Are there government grant programs?	Big emerging market; professionals love a credential and education self-improvement, go beyond a rep office—need to get official recognition; everything works by relationship
Japan	√	Not much	Courses and board member		Professionals love a credential self-improvement
W. Europe	√ Aging population	Considerable	Almost none: course in Vienna	There is sponsorship here, and the Association has gone after it	Oldest populations; tend to be anti-American

(*Continued*)

Table 6.1 (*Continued*)

Region/ Country	Total Potential as a Target Audience (Based on population, age, wealth, size)	Competition/ Allies	Current Association Presence	Potential Sponsorship	Other Considerations
E. Europe	√	Not much	Much interest in Poland and Romania	Probably; government grants might be available	Friendlier toward United States
Latin America	Youthful population	Not much	Much interest; have held courses, and looking at a scientific session in Brazil	There is interest here	Education and credentialing gaining importance, but not as much as Asia-Pacific
Middle East		Some	Have held programs in Lebanon, Jordan, and Saudi Arabia	Unsure	
Australia/ New Zealand		Some	Have held courses; gave seed money for a course	Unsure	
South Africa		None	None	Unsure	
India		None	None	Unsure	Highly educated population

Shaded region/country areas should be targeted first.

Once you have this information that you will have gathered through reliable secondary and primary market research, you should then be able to prioritize the markets according to size, growth potential, absence or presence of competitors, legal and cultural openness to foreign entrants into their market, and the amount of time and effort that will be required before you can expect to cover your costs. On this last point, your revenue sources could change over time. In other words, the revenues that you use to launch your overseas presence, such as government or private grants, could evolve into indigenous revenue sources that will make your overseas presence sustainable.

The next and final step in this process is to develop three-year business plans for your top target markets. It is important that you give yourself a realistic time frame. Unless you are a grant recipient, it is almost unheard of for any new venture to be able to cover its own costs in the first year.

Why all this emphasis on money? Because without some sort of revenues, you simply cannot have a sustainable program in any country.

The Fee-for-Service Model Migration

Twenty to thirty years ago the majority of associations derived up to 80 percent of their revenues from membership dues (according to the American Society of Association Executives). However, this scenario has begun to change in the past two decades. Younger people ceased joining organizations with the same enthusiasm as their parents, and when they did join, it grew harder to keep them. As a result, many membership organizations began to experience a graying of their membership base.

Associations have responded in part by seeking out revenue streams beyond membership and have been forced to do some self-reflection on the value of membership itself. For many associations, nondues revenue coming from nonmembers will grow increasingly important in the future.

Associations that recognized changes in the nation's socioeconomic structure, such as the fact that most people change jobs several times in their career, were quick to develop and promote those products and services the market was demanding. Certification and accreditation programs that help enhance employability and guarantee quality, for example, are now in demand. Also of premium value are the education and training programs that support them. Many of the associations that have done the best financially over the past 20 years have transformed themselves into centers of professional learning or places where industry and professional standards are defined.

Following are some trends in today's association landscape, each of which bears heavily on membership and revenue:

- *Networking means something different nowadays.* Potential members are more than ever lo.oking to associations as opportunities for networking. While networking has always been a draw for associations, now it often is valued as a job search tool first and foremost, whereas for prior generations networking simply meant meeting and forming bonds with people with similar values and interests.
- *Associations have become more specialized.* The International Institute for Real Estate Finance is a spin-off of the Mortgage Bankers Association of America; the National Coalition for Quality Diagnostic Imaging Services was created to represent a niche group: the manufacturers and users of magnetic resonance imaging.
- *Revenue flows have changed.* As much as 80 percent of a successful association's revenues now come from the sale of products and services. The IIA gets only 25 percent of its revenue come from dues.
- *Associations have had to learn to cultivate, promote, and protect their name brands in the same way as for-profit corporations.* The American Association of Snowboard Instructors was created as a brand within the Professional Ski Instructors of America for the simple reason that snowboarders have historically considered themselves a separate breed from skiers. Associations, in fact, have even had to compete increasingly with for-profit corporations entering fields that have been usually the reserve of nonprofit organizations. Organizations that have failed to adapt to this new environment have either become "clubs" of like-minded friends who meet for social purposes, or they have ceased to exist altogether.

Following are some tips that can help your organization succeed in this new climate:

- *Consider membership a gateway, not an end unto itself.* Membership in AARP—the largest membership organization—costs $12.50 a year in dues. Their principal interest is to provide valued products and services to their target market. In effect, the American Association of Retired Persons, Washington, D.C., charges only enough in membership dues to maintain members on mailing lists. The real revenues, and the fulfillment of the organization's mission, come from the kind and quality of products and services the organization delivers.

- *Revisit your strategy.* Review your strategic positioning in the market and your organization's relevance annually. A survey of Washington, D.C.-based associations found that most associations were doing a top-to-bottom strategic analysis of their operations annually.
- *Create value for your name brand.* As membership loyalty declines, people make their buying choices based on what they know and hear about name brands. This means that successful associations are much more attuned to the need for building and maintaining brand awareness—in much the same way as the for-profit world operates. The CPA of the American Institute of Certified Public Accountants is a good example of a certification "product" that has developed remarkable brand recognition in this country and around the world.
- *Define your target audience and know their needs and concerns.* Many associations make more sales to people and organizations that are not members than those who are, even when there is a financial advantage to being a member. For example, the Project Management Institute, Newtown Square, Pennsylvania, one of the nation's fastest-growing associations in terms of revenue, derives as much of its product and service revenue from nonmembers as from members.

With membership loyalty largely being a thing of the past, associations must develop cutting-edge products and services that can compete in increasingly crowded markets. Levels of both nondues revenue and sales to nonmembers can serve as an indication of your association's future relevance.

These practices work well—indeed are critical—in successful international market development.

Chapter 7

Successes and Failures

Key Ingredients to Globalization Success

Fortunately, an experienced base—consisting of both successes and failures—is emerging to reveal certain patterns from which we can learn. This chapter includes case studies exemplifying successes and failures in globalization. It identifies four models and their comparative advantages and disadvantages in four categories of global markets. Finally, it discusses the problems associated with globalization and how a variety of associations successfully dealt with them.

Action Plans for Globalization Success

Following are some actions that, performed well, will give associations a better chance of establishing globalization efforts that work.

- *Determine need.* An effective strategy starts with the realization that globalization is both a threat and an opportunity. The wise association executive will quantify what these threats and opportunities are and how they relate to the local needs and concerns of the association's members. Determining the need (or opportunity) will also help to identify the appropriate business model to best respond, that is, international, multinational and multilocal, or truly global models.

- *Identify value to current members.* Once association leaders decide to adopt an active approach toward the globalization trends that surround them, they need to take care that their actions bring value to members and customers—and that includes creating a positive impact on the association's bottom line. As powerful and important as globalization is in the abstract, no stakeholder will or should tolerate either deficit spending or the proliferation of products and services that are irrelevant to the organization's mission.
- *Be creative: look beyond dues for financing.* There is no organization in the world that can deliver something for nothing—but don't look toward dues to find your financing answers to international initiatives. For one thing, what is fair dues assessment for an American member may be unfair for a Chinese member. As with most domestic nonprofit organizations these days, successful global operations focus on designing and delivering valuable products and services that result in the vast majority of their revenues being derived from such nondues sources. Nondues revenues are a powerful tool toward achieving the organization's mission, enabling the organization to do far more than with dues revenues alone. Positive financing issues underscore the necessity of any organization to offer value to its members.

It is also worth noting the importance of including annual research and development financing in the annual operational budget. Successful organizations sustain their success through continuous annual research and development (R&D), bringing new and revised goods and services to their markets. Organizations that do the same thing, year after year, have a hard time keeping up with the changes going on around them. A number of organizations "earmark" a portion of their reserve funds to support proposals for new innovation and entrepreneurial activities, such as globalization. These proposals may be submitted quarterly to a review panel authorized to dispense funds to approved proposals, thus stimulating a constant flow of new ideas from all directions.

- *Get the governance right.* To truly understand how complicated democracy is, try putting together an effective global governance structure. Associations going global need to carefully match the governance model to the business model, and the organization's mission and goals, taking into account memberships, head counts, national origins, and the relative levels of contributions of each identifiable group to an organization's operations. The one-country/one-vote approach of the United Nations does not work in the private or nongovernmental organization sectors, nor does a one person, one vote approach. Minority opinions do matter, and nothing will undermine an association more quickly than to have the same minority group's opinion overlooked again and again. This is particularly true if the minority happens to be the one that pays most of the bills.

  For organizations that seek to be entrepreneurial and innovative, a "top-down," command and control organization governance may not be the most conducive to "crazy ideas" bubbling up from all parts of a diverse and global organization. Governance, business model, and organizational mission and goals need to be very much in sync.
- *Manage cultural and professional differences.* Most associations' leaders know that treating members and customers with tender loving care is an essential component of successful association management. This is all the more true when ethnic, religious, linguistic, and cultural differences are added to the membership mix. In the world of international affairs, such differences create a volatile mix that can—and does—cause wars; imagine what they can do to an association. In that light, the cultural sensitivity of the association staff and volunteer leaders who are on the front lines is absolutely critical to the initial and ongoing success of any operation that aspires to have global reach. If you handle each of these key areas with care, you increase the odds that your organization's globalization efforts will meet with success.

Similarly, the organization's business model must provide the same care, respect, and value to local members and customers, throughout the global reach of the organization's operations. Cross-border organizations must be concerned with effective pricing and distribution methods. Multinational and multilocal organizations, however, must be concerned not just with pricing and distribution, but also must give critical attention to local member and customer service (often in the host-country language and currency) customization of goods and services and local governance participation and controls. Truly global organizations must "think locally" and be highly networked with decisions made at globally distributed centers of competence. Regardless of organizational goals and business model, cultural and professional differences must be met successfully.

Over the past decade, increasing numbers of U.S.-based associations have responded to the needs of their members outside of North America as well as to growing demand worldwide for credentialing and the type of professional training and education programs they offer. Some associations have responded passively by serving only the foreign markets that come to them, but those organizations that have benefited most from globalization are those that have developed proactive approaches in which they tailor-make and deliver the types of products and services needed to select overseas markets. The following report consists of case studies that describe the various successful methodologies that have been used in this proactive approach as well as their relative strengths and weaknesses for each type of overseas market.

A Look at Four Models

There are four models that offer different sets of strengths and weaknesses depending on the organizations' mission and goals, resulting in the type of product and service offered and according to the type and level of development of the overseas market. In developing these market penetration strategies, every association has had to come to grips with two issues:

1. *Structure.* How do you position your organization to offer value in terms of any sister organizations outside the United States? Are those associations' rivals or allies? Chances are, they do not fit comfortably in either category. If they cannot be embraced

entirely, neither can they be ignored. What strategic options are available for structuring your presence abroad?

2. *Funding*. Members generally want their dues used for products, programs, and services that benefit them, not to benefit other national markets. So where can you find the funds to create or grow a global organization? And, once found, how can you ensure that your members see the value of new global activities?

Fortunately, association X has multiple models to choose from in addressing both the structuring and funding challenges, as the following four examples illustrate.

Model One: Networking International Subsidiaries and Chapters

One of the best ways to expand globally, deal with potential overseas competitors, and provide a seamless global service delivery system for members or customers with global needs is to create a tightly woven networked subsidiary, chapter, or affiliate network that serves the local market but also is closely integrated into a global operation. One successful example is in the corporate world—Deloitte Touche Tohmatsu, a global accounting and management consulting partnership.

In the early 1990s, Deloitte evaluated the economic globalization trends of its corporate market and determined that the best way to attract new customers and avoid losing others to competitors was to create a seamless global structure.

Transforming a loosely affiliated network of partnerships with different names, cultures, languages, laws, and traditions was no easy matter. But what drove the process was the belief that each aspect of the firm would, in the end, stand to benefit financially. With local clients already in place, the promise of more business through the growing need of multinational clients for integrated global services made it easier to bear the five years of costs and compromises required to create the global firm that Deloitte is today.

In this structure, each local element is a legal and financial entity unto itself, thus ensuring limited financial and legal exposure for the other parts of the global firm should anything go wrong. Each entity became part of the global organization through the laws of a Swiss *verein*, which is the equivalent of a loosely affiliated trade association or guild through which the members agree to work together in certain ways. Any disputes among these elements were to be sorted out through regional coordinating bodies and, if necessary, the world governing body. Managing partners of the largest firms in each region comprised that global governing body.

Deloitte established teams to develop and deliver global services to customers, wherever they may be. This introduced an important new profit-center concept based on global customer service, rather than one rooted in any given national market. The national entities welcomed this, because the global service teams drew on the resources of each respective national operation, and this produced revenue for everyone.

To further fuel the creation of this global entity, Deloitte bid on service contracts offered by the World Bank and U.S. Agency for International Development (USAID), which needed accounting, auditing, and managing services in developing markets worldwide. As Deloitte won such contracts in central and eastern Europe and in the People's Republic of China, it used the new revenue streams to establish national operations in each new market where it had gained a foothold.

New Deloitte offices in Moscow, Beijing, and elsewhere were 100 percent funded in the first few years of their existence through the programs they were running for the World Bank and USAID. The bigger goal, though, was to use these contracts as opportunities to find on-the-ground customers who would permit the offices to continue once the international lending agency funding gave out. In every instance, they were successful in doing so. (This case study is further developed under a different angle under Issue 4, discussed later).

Deloitte fashioned a truly global organization in which:

- Products and services are flexible and could be customized for either local or global conditions.
- The business model is highly networked and distributed around the world.
- The basis of value and competition focuses on economies of scale for production and knowledge, while innovation is locally driven.

- Organization and staffing decisions are made at globally distributed centers of competence, with provision for dispute resolution.
- Customers are supported both globally and locally by "thinking-locally" models.

Model Two: Developing a Global Federation

Throughout its long existence as a professional society, the Institute of Internal Auditors (IIA) had helped foster the creation and growth of multiple national sister organizations around the world. As it did so, many members of these sister organizations also joined the U.S.-based IIA.

These developments were mostly positive, but such success created problems of a special kind. Because non-American members paid less for membership than U.S. members, U.S. members of the IIA increasingly complained that they were bearing an unfair proportion of the costs for running programs and activities outside the United States. The non-American members, however, were aware of their own numbers and questioned why the IIA governance structure was so heavily biased toward Americans.

After engaging all parties in an extensive strategic planning exercise, the IIA developed a federated global structure. National entities remained the primary service providers to their respective national markets; a global IIA provided services in the areas of networking, certification and training, and standards development—each of which everyone agreed served widespread need and demand.

The revenues derived from these services constitute most of the funding required to run the global operations. However, to complement these revenues, the IIA also adopted the same strategy deployed by Deloitte Touche Tohmatsu: bidding on international market development projects funded by the World Bank and USAID. As the IIA wins these international lending agency projects, it generates revenues for the global operation and the national entities that contribute project resources. It also has succeeded in creating new IIA members in these developing markets, some of which have developed their own national IIA organizations.

Such a federated structure has many of the same advantages of a chapter or subsidiary structure but with fewer direct costs and less central control. (This case study is further developed under a different angle under Issue 4, discussed later).

In this example of a multinational and multilocal organization:

- Products and services are largely homogeneous, with some customization locally.
- The business model is highly duplicated in each country, with country independence.
- The basis of value and competition combines key centralized innovation from home country with local country innovation and tailoring.
- Organization and staffing is rooted in local markets but with global accountability.
- Customers are primarily local, regardless of global location.

Model Three: Global Strategic Alliances

The American Oil Chemists Society (AOCS) and National Osteoporosis Foundation (NOF) are both nonprofit organizations that pride themselves on their American roots, but both also have widespread interests beyond U.S. boundaries. To accommodate the diverse interests and origins of their global participants, both organizations have developed extensive networks of strategic partnerships overseas. These partnerships consist of cooperation and joint venture agreements with a wide variety of other types of organizations to host international conferences and other information exchanges. Revenue-sharing arrangements are worked out on a project-by-project basis for jointly sponsored conference.

Such alliances offer maximum flexibility to partner with organizations that may share some of the same interests but that otherwise are very different. In such arrangements it is not uncommon to have partnerships with organizations representing governmental and academic entities, as well as for-profit and other nonprofit organizations. Global alliances are easier to put together and even less expensive to operate than a global federation, but they also afford less control or shared sense of purpose than either of the other two organizational types noted previously. Such structures are ideal for nationally rooted organizations that want to remain tied to international trends and developments but that lack the resources or driving incentive to develop permanent operations beyond their own borders.

In this example of a global exporter, or cross-border organization:

- Products and services tend to be homogeneous with modest customization for global customers.
- Business structure is highly concentrated in the home country.
- Basis of value and competition is addressed through economies of scale in home-country production and distribution coupled with host-country cooperation and support on a project basis.
- Organization and staffing is primarily by home-country nationals, aided by host-country organizations and staff on a project basis.
- Customers are treated largely the same, and largely pay the same, whether global or local.

Model Four: A Technology-Reliant Global Network

Like most professional societies and even trade associations, the members and board of the Society of Human Resource Management (SHRM) traditionally saw their mission and goals and defined their interests in terms of their domestic national market. Consequently, it was difficult for SHRM staff to justify spending more than a nominal amount of time and money on products or services outside of the United States. Nevertheless, this did not prevent SHRM from developing a model global organization based primarily on use of the Internet.

SHRM found that its sister organizations abroad had a high level of interest in its programs and activities. Accordingly, it developed memoranda of understanding that allowed each sister organization to offer their members access to SHRM's products and services via the Internet as a membership benefit. In return for offering password-protected access to the members of sister societies abroad, SHRM also offered to host or link with websites offered by those sister societies in their own languages.

Such an arrangement has constituted a "virtual" global organization for SHRM and its members while keeping costs to a minimum. In fact, the revenue-sharing arrangements SHRM has negotiated with sister organizations has produced a modest but positive net contribution to the society's bottom line.

This is an example of "electronic" globalization using what appears to be a global exporter or "cross-border" model.

Making the Choice

These four structural models are not mutually exclusive. In other words, choosing one does not mean you cannot employ variations of other models at the same time. This is what IIA did. Indeed, on a project-by-project basis, it may be possible for one organization to simultaneously use all four models for international expansion at the same time, depending on the opportunities and challenges encountered. In effect, these models represent some of the tools available to creative association leaders who recognize the need to grapple with the reality of a global economy on a case-by-case basis—where country situations and projects may vary. Thus, there may be no single universal solution that will fit every situation that is encountered.

It is a mistake to think that because an organization is nonprofit, it is not or should not be concerned about profitable operations. While money may not be the only success measure of a nonprofit organization, it is a necessary ingredient for successful longevity. Money is what subsidizes goods and services that are essential to the organizational mission, but for which the same goods and services may have little revenue-producing potential. Since dues revenue, in and of itself, cannot usually support all of the desired goods and services of the organization, nondues revenues, from revenue-producing goods and services, is a major source of organizational strength. Thus, money can be a useful measuring stick for determining the popularity and usefulness of any given activity, regardless of whether the activity is subsidized or revenue producing. In the case of these four models, the revenue drivers come from one or more of three sources—customers, members, or sponsors who have a financial interest in the success of your undertaking; government funds (as in the case of international lending agency programs); and joint financial ventures in which costs and revenues are split with participating organizations.

Not every organization has equal access to each of these possible revenue streams, but everyone has potential access to at least one. Your only limit to global growth is one imposed by your own imagination.

Costs versus Benefits of Each Model in Four Overseas Market Categories

There are a number of markets that presented strong opportunities for association X globalization initiatives. Broadly speaking, these (and other markets) can be separated into four broad groups, namely, developed economies, big emerging markets, developing markets, and least developed markets.

We have analyzed the costs and risks versus the benefits of each model as it is applied to each of association X's four potential market categories. In effect, we are using a matrix analytical structure, as shown in Table 7.1.

Developed Economies

Developed economies are the world's largest, most mature and stable economies. These markets present obvious attractions but they also

Table 7.1 Globalization Matrix

Strategic Models: Market Category:	One (International Subsidiaries and Chapters)	Two (Global Federation)	Three (Global Strategic Alliances)	Four (Technology-Linked Global Network)
1. Developed economies—Canada, western Europe, and Japan[a]				
2. Big emerging markets—China, Russia, India, and Brazil[a,b]				
3. Developing markets—e.g., Mexico, Singapore, South Korea, Taiwan, South Africa, and Argentina[a,b]				
4. Least developed markets—e.g., Republic of Georgia, Peru[b]				

[a] Corporate funds

[b] Development agency fund

have relatively low growth rates and offer more competition than is usually found in other market categories.

Model One: International Subsidiaries and Chapters. *Costs/risks:* High level of competition from existing professional societies may drain away any potential of finding a critical mass of membership to create self-sustaining operations and may create antagonism with those societies. Some initial subsidization may be required to start operations that appear viable.

Benefits: This could be used as a way to serve the professional training and credentialing needs of those U.S. corporations that are heavily invested in these markets (as noted above). It may also serve as a way to leverage association X's standards and programs into markets that have established themselves as rivals.

Model Two: Global Federation. *Costs/risks:* Harmonizing differences between standards and programs of the various societies may prove insurmountable, but the costs would be mostly in the time and travel expenses of the association X executive that would take on this matchmaking responsibility.

Benefits: The benefits of such an approach could be great—if association X uses Model One as a strategy to leverage cooperation and concessions to create Model Two. This approach was used successfully by the Association of Career Management Consulting Firms International (AOCFI) to negotiate a federated structure with their European counterparts. The alternative they offered the Europeans was to set up their own parallel chapters in Europe.

Model Three: Global Strategic Alliances. *Costs/risks:* The only cost in pursuing this approach is in the time and travel costs of the association X executive(s) who would take on this assignment. There are no risks other than that failure to create such alliances would result in losing this investment in time and money.

Benefits: Association X's key to success in these national markets is to integrate itself as a fully recognized national player and not as an American interloper. This model, in combination with Models One and/or Two, will help achieve this end. However, without recourse to one of the two previous models, association X will continue to be viewed as an American entity, and this will necessarily limit its influence in these markets.

Model Four: Technology-Linked Global Network. *Costs/risks:* The key is to explore whether association X's sister organizations in this market would welcome association X hosting a global website through which they could sell benefits to their members. The purpose of this approach is to offer a value-added service that sister organizations can in turn sell to their membership. As in the case of SHRM, association X could offer a package of services that would be priced and whose costs would be shared by all those participating in the project. There may be some up-front costs for developing showcase concepts.

The only risk would be in cannibalizing participation in association X's own programs or in compromising its intellectual property rights. Such risks can and should be covered under the contractual language that association X would use in this venture.

Benefits: To create communications channels and tangible service exchanges with sister societies and through this, to create a virtual global network in support of mechanical engineers in the world's largest markets.

Big Emerging Markets (BEMs)

The BEMs have the highest growth rates and offer the greatest long-term potential of any market due to their size. However, instability is sometimes an issue.

Model One: International Subsidiaries and Chapters. *Costs/risks:* Association X would have greater ease in setting up chapters or subsidiaries in such countries due to the lesser sophistication of the societies that are there, but with considerable risk that these operations could prove to be a financial drain on association X's resources. To limit these risks, it will be important to design a business plan that clearly defines what association X will provide and what resources must be found by the local operation. In this regard, since these markets are the preferred destination of many corporations, programs could be designed around these corporate needs with corporate funds serving to fuel this effort to transfer association X know-how into these markets.

In some instances, international government-sponsored programs might be found and used as a platform from which to build association X's on-the-ground operations.

Benefits: Establishing association X's presence in the world's fastest-growing markets.

Model Two: Global Federation. *Costs/risks:* If this model were to be pursued, it would be an unbalanced relationship because association X is far larger and more sophisticated than any sister society currently existing in these markets. The costs for maintaining this structure therefore would be disproportionately great for association X, unless it is structured carefully with association X as a service provider to the societies in these countries—with these services being paid for on a cash basis. Governmental grants might be available, but there would likely be insufficient self-interest for corporations to be interested in funding this approach.

Benefits: Such a model would lock association X into a supplier relationship and in effect position itself as a mentor for fostering the growth of the mechanical engineering societies in these national markets.

Model Three: Global Strategic Alliances. This model would carry the same costs/risks and benefits as Model Two.

Model Four: Technology-Linked Global Network. *Costs/risks:* These markets are large users of association X's website. There may be some interest in pursuing this linkage with association X, but the financial resources this would generate would be limited. These markets would likely also have a greater need for translations into their native languages—something they should do for themselves using association X materials. Care needs to be taken to protect association X's intellectual property rights.

Benefits: The long-term potential benefits could be great, but a quick return on investment would be unlikely. However, the costs and risks of this approach would be minimal if structured prudently.

Developing Markets

These markets have both great growth potential and great risk. They deserve scrutiny on a case-by-case basis.

Model One: International Subsidiaries and Chapters. *Costs/risks:* Association X may need to invest in start-up costs, and care should be taken to ensure intellectual property right and name-brand protection for association X–generated products and materials.

These markets would not qualify for major government-funded projects, but they do attract corporate trade and investment. It is through this latter source that association X could explore subsidization opportunities.

Nationality requirements may require association X to set up a separate legal entity that would need to be majority owned by local nationals. In this case, association X should use some fail-safe legal mechanism that would guarantee respect for governance integrity and the mission and values of association X generally.

Benefits: This market category is likely to be very receptive to association X's approach and could offer both short- and long-term benefits in growing membership outside North America.

Model Two: Global Federation. *Costs/risks:* Working with societies that exist in these national markets, association X could create a federated structure through which it can channel and sell its products and services. The advantage to this approach for this market is that nationalistic considerations may cause societies to prefer to deal with an American organization like association X through the veil of a global structure. If so, this approach could entail some up-front investment in time and possible legal costs to set up this tiered approach.

Benefits: The benefits from this model would be mostly long term, so it will be important for association X to closely control its up-front costs by adopting a minimalist approach.

Model Three: Global Strategic Alliances. This model would probably not be appropriate for developing markets.

Model Four: Technology-Linked Global Network. *Costs/risks:* These markets may represent a good alliance partner for this approach either by itself or in conjunction with Model Two. Neither costs nor risks would be great—provided translating costs be made the responsibility of the national markets requesting this service.

There may be some corporate funding interest from those multinationals that have targeted these markets.

Benefits: The benefits would be modest, but over the long term it could offer a good foothold for association X and a possible valued service for association X corporate customers.

Least Developed Markets

These markets are and should be attractive to those associations that are used to working with bilateral and multilateral development agencies. Through such programs there is little risk and great satisfaction in doing well by doing good.

This market is open to approaches represented by all the models insofar as they fit the requirements of the government-funded program(s) that would finance them. As corporate interests in this market category are minimal, bilateral and multilateral government-funded projects are the only driving forces that could carry association X's activities into these countries.

Four Issue Areas

In light of these examples, we now examine how association X can best address the four issue areas:

1. Tailor-making and protecting association X's ownership rights over the types of intellectual property—products and services—that overseas markets want and need.
2. Focusing association X's existing operational structures in a way that mitigates or eliminates their working at cross-purposes with each other in the international marketplace.
3. Developing association X's corporate membership concept and turning it into a marketing tool for developing association X's presence overseas.

4. Developing a governance and operational structure that accommodates the special needs of these overseas markets and reflects their importance for association X.

All associations, as they expand from domestic to international to multinational to global, find it useful to use one or more combinations of the models as described in Table 7.1. On a more tactical level, following are four common issues that most associations face when they expand globally, as described in four case studies of associations that successfully navigated these challenges.

Issue 1

Lack of intellectual property (IP), IP protection, and comprehensive incentive-based royalty system for encouraging the use of association X products and services is the first issue addressed in the following case study.

AFP Expands Certification Program Globally. The Association for Financial Professionals (AFP), formerly the Treasury Management Association, has grown in the past 20 years into a community of more than 14,000 individuals representing a broad spectrum of financial disciplines. AFP turns knowledge into performance by supporting members throughout all stages of their careers with research, continuing education, career development, professional certifications, publications, representation to key legislators and regulators, and the development of industry standards.

The Challenge

How could AFP introduce and promote its certification program overseas?

AFP's *Certified Cash Manager (CCM) credential program* is regarded by financial professionals as one of the leading certification programs in the field. Nearly 13,000 global financial professionals currently hold this credential. Understanding that English was the "language of finance" and that standards were needed to promote global commerce, AFP's staff was searching for an opportunity to expand the program and their services to other, specifically foreign, markets.

The Solution

AFP licensed its certification program to and built a successful alliance with an international, allied association.

The AFP licensed its CCM credential program to the Japan Association for Chief Financial Officers (JACFO). The credential program now provides the benchmark standard in cash management for Japanese financial officers.

With the help of technology, such as email and the Internet, AFP has been able to establish a joint venture alliance with JACFO. The Japanese professionals realized that companies "in country" were changing and that lifetime employment was no longer guaranteed. They also realized that certification plays an important role in career development and advancement and that they should take advantage of the growing global market. AFP saw this as an opportunity to expand its "global brand" and build a successful alliance for both parties.

The Process

The JACFO promotes exchanges with related foreign institutions and organizations, fostering the CFOs with knowledge, skills, and ethical principles, with an overall mission to develop global standards for financial management in Japan.

The JACFO first visited AFP at its annual conference last fall. This event attracted more than 6,500 participants and 300 exhibitors.

The entire process was quite lengthy, and the parties developed more than ten contract drafts within a span of four to five months. Some of the issues that were addressed included:

- Copyright and intellectual property laws
- Translation of certification materials, including the marketing materials, application, and Candidate Information Bulletin
- Protection and use of the actual brand name and symbol
- Customizing the product to Japanese practices

AFP had already developed the content and practices for managing the CCM program. JACFO was responsible for translating the program materials and tests into Japanese for use and administration of the CCM program to its members. In addition, JACFO was charged with developing additional test questions and materials to test an individual's knowledge of Japanese cash management practices.

JACFO was also expected to pay a small licensing fee for the program. However, they were expected to make a significant investment in the test development and building the CCM brand. The test development process lasts approximately one year and includes an exam that would be offered the following spring or summer.

Meeting and Negotiation Process

This was a day-to-day process that greatly depended on technology such as email. There also was a U.S. contact in Baltimore who was fluent in English and greatly helped the process. Most of the negotiation was done through conference calls; technology once again was a vital facilitating factor in helping to cultivate the relationship between AFP and JAFCO.

During the negotiation phase, JAFCO representatives came to the United States one month into the process of the agreement, and the two parties met two additional times. There were approximately 100 hours spent on the project with two people from AFP. Outsourced legal counsel negotiated the principles of the contract.

Some of the issues covered during the negotiation phase included:

- Use of the printed logo and brand
- Intellectual property rights
- Dispute resolution
- Tiered structure royalty agreement

Japan is the second-largest economy in the world. Given this fact, it was very important for AFP to maintain the integrity of the certification process, while at the same time trying to negotiate with JACFO.

Outsourcing

The Chauncey Group International, a subsidiary of Educational Testing Service (ETS) and the testing vendor, is working directly with JACFO to translate the CCM body of knowledge and test materials as well as all aspects of test development. Once the exam is ready to administer, JACFO will work with Chauncey's Japanese partner, the Institute for International Business Communications (IIBC), which handles all test administration. The IIBC is the same group that administers the TOEIC (Test of English for International Communications) exam in Japan.

Unforeseen Benefits

There were many benefits for AFP that resulted from the strategic alliance with the JACFO. Some of these included:

- The founder of the Japanese Association, Hiroshi Yaguchi, appointed AFP's president and CEO, Jim Kaitz, to serve on its board of directors.
- An article concerning this alliance appeared in *Nikkei*, one of the most prestigious and largest economic papers in Japan.
- There was a large response, following a press release announcing the alliance, from many financial institutions, accounting offices, corporate finance departments, and several educational companies to cooperate with JACFO on this venture.
- Hitachi Capital Corporation and NEC have introduced the CCM program into their own treasury departments.
- The Institute of Certified Public Accountants offered to introduce the CCM program as a continuing education course, sponsored by the Japan Chamber of Commerce and Industry.
- LEC, one of the largest educational companies in the business field in Japan, offered to help plan the administration of the CCM program.

In addition, AFP is currently working toward a CCM licensing agreement with the Korea CFO Association. This alliance may include the sharing of information such as AFP publications. Building partnerships with countries in Asia has helped build and promote AFP's brand and its services.

Lessons Learned

The most important element that was learned was the importance in creating a lasting bond with the Japanese professionals in the same industry. The language barrier was not so much an issue compared to the importance of understanding the Japanese culture and one of its key tenets that you build business on relationships and patience. The agreement between the two parties was the first crucial step; however, the importance of negotiation, patience, and understanding is what made this joint alliance truly successful.

Issue 2

Lack of market restriction clauses in chapter and affiliate agreements, leading to possible turf conflicts and the lack of rules of engagement regarding how to develop association X in countries outside the United States, make up the second issue, which is discussed in the case study that follows.

Society for Human Resource Management (SHRM) Expands Its Membership Internationally. SHRM membership consists of almost 600 U.S. chapters and more than 235,000 members (professionals).

SHRM is the largest nonprofit organization of its kind in the world and the global voice of the human resource profession. Over five thousand of its members are from outside the United States. These members joined SHRM despite there not being any direct marketing or recruiting effort outside the United States. The largest number of non-U.S. members comes from Canada, India, the Middle East, and the rest of Asia. In all, SHRM's international membership covers 105 countries.

The Challenge

How to provide effective service to international members with different cultural backgrounds and how to work effectively with affiliated organizations around the world?

As the international segment of SHRM's membership grew strongly, SHRM's management questioned how the Society could serve them better. The two main issues were:

- The logistics of serving an international membership with different languages and cultural backgrounds
- How SHRM should relate to its sister societies around the world

Logistics

The logistics problems were considerable. SHRM's international members received the same membership mailings as U.S. members. By the time the overseas members received them by mail delivery, they were often dated. And the cost of mailing the monthly magazine and newspaper nearly met the annual membership dues. How could these materials be more useable and timely, yet remain affordable?

Affiliate Relationships

There was also the issue that many of these overseas members came from countries where professional associations for human resource managers already existed. The question then was should SHRM even try to be more active in serving member needs in these markets? Wouldn't this be seen to be encroaching on the "turf" of its sister organizations? Related to this concern was the existence of the World Federation of Personnel Management Associations (WFPMA), a group of 55 HR associations from around the world. How would SHRM's global activities be interpreted by this group, of which SHRM was a member and also served as president, from 1998 to 2000?

The Solution

SHRM changed its bylaws and dues structure to accommodate global members and developed an effective Internet communications program to meet the information needs of international members.

The Process

Following are the steps that SHRM took to implement its global outreach program. Recognizing both the importance and the sensitivity of international issues:

- SHRM changed the bylaws to introduce a global member category.
- SHRM's board of directors approved the new laws in November 1997.
- SHRM global members are required to:
  - Pay dues to SHRM.
  - Reside outside the United States.

- Belong to the local/national human resource association (where one existed).
- Receive all the printed publications of SHRM online—no physical mail.

Taking on this project newly into his tenure, the vice president for international programs identified two key objectives:

1. Define how this new area of activity would fit within SHRM's structure, programs, and services.
2. Determine how Global Forum would relate to other personnel management associations abroad, including the WFPMA.

Both internal and external considerations were taken into account.

Internal Structure

With regard to internal structure, it was determined that this new initiative would:

- Establish an global advisory committee (selected according to professional status, abilities and geographic representation) to provide vision and guidance.
- Require a separate, firewalled SHRM Global Forum website to separate the Internet-based publications from the domestic SHRM members.
- Encompass the activities and website of the previously existing Institute for International Human Resources (IIHR), which was formed in 1991.

The IIHR consisted of 6,000 members, many of whom were U.S.- based, who had an interest in international or global issues. The SHRM Global Forum would thus build on this base and expand the level of web-based products to the membership.

External Considerations

How the SHRM Global Forum would relate to other overseas organizations still remained to be resolved, but it was felt that first they needed to address the logistics of how SHRM's current 2,000 overseas members could be better served. For this, SHRM turned to technology:

- SHRM determined that virtually all their target audience had Internet access.
- They constructed a password-protected website through which all members of the Global Forum could access the latest publications and communicate among themselves.
- They marketed the Global Forum to counterpart organizations.
- They encouraged counterpart organizations to have their members join the SHRM Global Forum in return for a rebate for each member recruited.
- They adopted a rule that no overseas member could join if they did not first belong to their own national or regional organization.
- They structured collaborative agreements with international counterpart organizations to offer cooperative programming such as seminars or exchange of content.

By using the web, SHRM was able to offer lower membership fees for these Internet-only international members, except for those members still wanting to receive hard copies of all publications.

A Collaborative Effort

In order to reassure overseas sister organizations that SHRM did not intend to compete for their members, the SHRM Global Forum adopted the rule that no overseas member could join if they did not first belong to their own national or regional organization. Also, in the promotional brochures created for the SHRM Global Forum, the supportive relationship of SHRM to other international organizations—particularly those within the WFPMA—was clearly defined so that there would be no confusion or misperception as to the nature of SHRM's global activities.

The entire process of creating SHRM's Global Forum can be described as "collaborative." The creation of new internal staffing was kept to a minimum. The international VP's role was not to recreate what already existed with SHRM's many departments but rather to work with these departments in adapting existing and developing new products and services that were sensitive to the needs of international members, specifically with regards to their online applicability.

Measurements and Results

"5,000 global members in five years"

Ultimately, the results of SHRM's Global Forum will be measured by international membership statistics. To date, SHRM has made a significant financial commitment to Global Forum and is optimistic about the anticipated results of the effort. The SHRM Global Forum initiative has required SHRM to make a financial investment in technology and staff that may not be recovered for several years. This decision to invest in the international development of the organization is testimony to the health of the organization, as well as the belief of its leadership in SHRM's global potential.

SHRM hopes to have 5,000 members outside the United States in five years. But there is also the recognition that globalization requires a slow process of relationship building, and that patience and having a long-term perspective will be essential to the Global Forum's success.

Lessons Learned

In developing a global program, SHRM learned the following lessons:

- In introducing global programs, almost as much attention needs to be paid to the internal education and training of an organization's staff and volunteer leadership as to the development of the programs themselves.
- Relationship building is key to success in overseas markets that are wary of the size and intentions of their larger U.S. counterpart organizations.
- A certain amount of time and financial resources need to be invested before such an effort can be expected to pay for itself. The primary motivating factor behind a drive toward globalization is not and should not be financial.
- Successful globalization means opening an organization's decision-making processes as well as its products and services to global influences.

- Creating and empowering an international staff function within an organization may serve as a useful first step in helping it to become global.

Issue 3

The lack of a strategic partnership model to facilitate membership growth abroad is the third issue demonstrated in the International Society for Clinical Densitometry (ISCD) case study.

ISCD Develops Global Approach Concepts and Considerations. The International Society for Clinical Densitometry, a U.S.-based professional membership society, found itself at a crossroads. It did not promote itself as an international organization, but it had not found a way to attract any significant numbers for international membership or global education. It determined that it needed to develop a model or models to accomplish this. The model they developed was based on partnering with locally based sister organizations and/or corporations or governmental entities. They determined that these entities were the most cost-effective method to penetrate and deliver services in local markets abroad.

In 2006, 93 percent of ISCD members were based in the United States. Seven percent were located in other countries, with approximately half of those residing in Canada. ISCD dues were increased for 2007.

Over the past three years, concern had been raised about the cost of services and products paid by ISCD members in the United States and other countries. Attempts at alternative pricing structures had been generally rejected by the ISCD membership committee, except for a 2003 policy setting a dual membership for SOLAD (Latin America) members. Concern had been raised from non–North American countries about the high cost of ISCD programs and services. These concerns were raised most notably from Asian and Latin American countries.

To address the issue, the ISCD board of directors created and directed an International Relations Committee to bring forth a global approach to cost structures that would provide an incentive for organizations to partner with them while ensuring ISCD's costs would be covered. The charge given was to develop a global approach to provide a structure that would be objective, thus eliminating the need or inclination to negotiate special rates for countries or groups.

Following is an outline of their approach in their own words.

Executive Summary

Any relationship outside of North America should accomplish the following:

- ISCD should control the use of its logo and materials.
- ISCD will have marketing partners with these entities. In fact, we feel that an arrangement can be made so that revenue is shared by both entities.
- Staff time might be better used to work with these entities on the local scene rather than trying to do what they can do best locally. We do feel that we need one staff person or at least a part of one to work directly on this program.
- Dues and other fees could be collected locally and then remitted to ISCD with a list of names. We could look into electronic access as well.
- Possible sponsorship could be sought at the local level to cover the selected level.

We propose addressing our global collaborations in a manner that addresses ISCD cost based on what the partnering entity is able to do administratively. We see two main forms of collaboration:

1. *Full service.* ISCD provides full service to the local entity: ISCD processes membership, dues, registrations, maintains a section on the ISCD website. Course registration would be processed locally.
2. *Limited service.* A menu of required services would be worked out and priced accordingly. The partnering entity could collect the money and remit only the ISCD portion. If it wanted to keep some funds for its operation, that certainly would be acceptable.

   The full range of services would include data entry of members, dues invoicing and processing, both print and the electronic version of the journal, maintenance of a section on the website, course registration, and so forth. Certain benefits might be awarded to full service such as complimentary registration to the annual meeting and membership on an international advisory board.

Based on the above and our research on other models, we feel that we can support the following concepts. In all cases, an agreement and program of work will be developed. All of this can be facilitated with a new membership system that will be implemented in the next six months. In the meantime, we feel that we can manage with our current process:

- That a China Panel be formed with a China office. The membership recruitment, development of materials, administration of courses will be directly through the China office and without significant ISCD expense. Chinese members of the China Panel will pay annual dues of $25 (clinician and technologist) to ISCD HQ. A charter will be developed in the next three months to delineate the required interactions between the China office and the ISCD HQ.
- That a category of membership be launched in Brazil and Argentina permitting co-membership with the local osteoporosis society and ISCD for an incremental fee of $100 (clinician and technologist) to be remitted in full to ISCD HQ. The membership management will be through ISCD HQ with ISCD expenses to be covered entirely by this fee. The membership will include electronic access to JCD and all other membership benefits. A charter will be developed in the next three months to delineate the required interactions between the LA Panel and the ISCD HQ.

We also feel that we can develop this program and provide a form of revenue sharing with the institution/organization. For example, if an entity exceeds their level requirements and sells more ISCD products or services, then a credit would be issued to them for that number times a percentage of our surplus.

Issue 4

Global issues are treated as a subset of North America—there is no provision for proportional representation by geographical sector on the board; and no service network or policy in place for serving the needs of distant members or members whose currency is not the U.S. dollar and whose first language is not English.

The Association of Career Management Consulting Firms International (AOCFI). Founded in the early 1980s, the AOCFI was a New Jersey–based trade association representing professional service firms in the booming outplacement industry. With its growing international membership, as well as its growing concern with the impact of legislation and regulations on its industry, its board of directors made the decision to relocate to Washington, D.C. From there it was felt the association would be better able to serve the interests of its international members, as well as tend to the government relations needs of its U.S. members. Although its membership covered over a dozen countries, the AOCFI's largest members were all U.S. companies, and most of its income in dues and services came from the United States as well. The second largest national market for membership was Canada.

This domination of North American members was normal in that the United States was the market that first "invented" the concept of outplacement, and it was the country that was furthest advanced in the development of professional practices and standards by which outplacement was defined. However, in the decade since the creation of the association, Europe had developed as the single fastest-growth market in the world for outplacement firms and services. By the mid-1990s, North America was seen to be mature with slow to flat growth prospects. "This was the reason the AOCFI board felt it needed to restructure itself—to give greater voice to the Europeans and to evolve from being an American-dominated, international association to one that was more "global in outlook and governance structure" said Frank Louchheim, founding chairman of Right Management Consulting and current member of the board of AOCFI.

They encountered three challenges:

1. *Standards.* Previously existing, small, nationally based outplacement trade associations in Europe had pretty much abandoned their efforts of trying to develop professional standards. The only

standards on which they could reach any membership consensus were so general and vague as to be meaningless. But if they were not satisfied with this result, they nevertheless resisted any attempt by the "American" association to saddle them with anything else.

2. *Dues.* The Europeans at one time paid dues at a different rate and in different ways than the Americans. To the Americans, the Europeans were not paying as much as U.S. members were. But the Europeans pointed out that they had many more diverse obligations at the national, regional, and world level than did the Americans and that if all their expenditures were taken into account, it would be seen that the Europeans were in fact paying more than the Americans.
3. *Identifying the value added of a new, global organization.* And, if there were increased costs associated with creating it, who would pay?

Despite this resistance, the AOCFI was able to obtain acceptance of its professional standards and even to reach agreement on a uniform international dues rate. It was able to override the objections of the European national associations because it determined there were enough members throughout the world who wanted uniform standards and dues that, if need be, the AOCFI could set up parallel operations in each national market if the existing associations did not concede. The AOCFI did not have to carry out this implied threat. The operations of the European organizations were merged into what was to be the newly federated structure of the AOCFI.

"Based on these major concessions," Louchheim said, "we rewrote the association's bylaws in which the governance structure of international, North America, Europe, and other parts of the world was redefined."

Because the membership was almost evenly split, it was agreed the worldwide presidency would alternate between North America and Europe. The worldwide board of directors was to be evenly split between North American and European representatives, and it was agreed that the board would always provide proportionate representation for every region of the world. In other words, as membership grew in Latin America and Asia-Pacific, the board would grow or reapportion itself as needed to allow for these new member voices to be heard in proportion to their numbers and financial contribution.

Since dues payments were standardized for all members no matter where they were based, the previous argument about financial contribution just went away. Dues are paid to the regional chapters, which at this point were Europe and North America. A small portion of these supports the oversight of AOCFI's international operations.

Apart from board representation noted earlier, the AOCFI's global organization was based on regions. Europe was a region as well as North America, and it was expected that Latin America and Asia-Pacific would develop their own regional structures as their membership expanded. The European regional operation was based in Brussels and run by a few full-time staff members. The North American region was based in Washington, D.C. Because North America was slightly larger than Europe, it was agreed that the international operations would continue to be based in Washington as well.

But the AOCFI had problems identifying the value added of any international or global services for its members. The newsletter was in English. Neither its language nor its primarily American content was deemed acceptable for most European markets—so the Europeans decided to create their own in addition to the one being done in North America. The association's professional standards were static and did not require any great maintenance. Virtually the only "international" product left was the annual international conference, which was, or should have been, self-supporting. The most important association service was government relations, but because this service was rendered on a national basis (with the exception of the lobbying done in Brussels on European Union issues), there was very little, if anything, that the international organization could contribute.

Budgets were developed at the national, regional, and global levels—in that order, based on need and on the amount of anticipated revenue from membership dues. What filtered up from the nations and regions to the global body was very little indeed.

Chapter 8

Final Thoughts on Truly Becoming Global

We have covered a lot of territory in the previous seven chapters. What have we learned? It would be nice if globalization were a finish line so that we could say to ourselves, "Here, finally, I have run the race, with considerable effort and sacrifice along the way, but now I can sit back and enjoy the laurels of victory." No such luck, unfortunately! Globalization defines an organizational structure and mind-set that can and does enhance or ensure the continued success of already successful organizations. Globalization also can offer new success in new markets for organizations that once were successful in markets that might now be in decline. But in all cases, a successful globalization effort is a continuous challenge. It needs to be built on an existing, solid base as defined by an organization with a vibrant mission and that is supported by products and services that respond to or that have the potential to respond to actual and evolving global market needs and wants.

The one constant in globalization is that it is a constantly shifting battlefield. Success attracts attention, and that attention leads to other organizations moving into your territory to share in your success! The one sure thing in all of this is that there will always be copycats popping up or organizations appearing that profess to have a better solution or better programs and products than what your organization is offering. As much as this may be hard to admit, all of this competition is good for consumers around the world—but that doesn't make your life as the provider any easier, does it?

Globalization is for the young at heart, because global players can never let their guard down, they can never give up trying to find new markets and better ways of doing things—ever. Whether you view this as a wearing struggle or a refreshing challenge is a matter of perspective and personality. But, like many things in life, optimists tend to have the long-term advantage when it comes to competing on the global stage. The pessimists just get too tired out to continue their struggles for long!

Nevertheless, the really scary thing about globalization is that you can't decide to opt out of it any more than you can decide not to breathe! The African story about the antelope and the lion comes to mind. The antelope knows that if it is to survive, it must be able to run and run fast. The lion knows that if it is to eat, it must be able to run and run fast to catch its meal. So at the dawn of every day, whether you are the antelope or the lion, you know you must be up and running to survive. Of course, globalization is like that—whether you decide to play an active or reactive role, you can't opt out of the game.

Globalization Is Survival: Becoming Global as an Antidote to Stagnant or Declining Markets

The Milwaukee-based American Society for Quality (ASQ) is an individual membership society made up of corporate quality control officers as well as consultants. During the heyday of the total quality management (TQM) frenzy of the 1960s through the 1990s, ASQ grew enormously fast. It bought and furnished its own building and filled it with the staff needed to serve a burgeoning membership base. But in the 1990s the novelty and sense of critical urgency of quality control started to wear off throughout the United States as corporations and management consultants turned their attentions elsewhere. This resulted in a gradual decline of ASQ's membership that continued unabated through 2007. With no end in sight for this decline that persisted over a decade whether the economy was strong or weak, ASQ's leadership decided that the time had come to look at markets outside the United States, which up to now had been considered as ancillary to their main interests.

ASQ prudently decided to research their options before choosing their path. They started by undertaking qualitative and quantitative market research starting with their overseas members. What they wanted to know was how they were perceived in markets outside the United States. Which products and services were most desired, which other organizations they were competing with in these various markets, and how their governance and operational structures were perceived in terms of their efficacy and relevancy to the needs and concerns of these markets.

What they found out was both good and bad. The good news was that their products and services fit very well with the needs of most overseas markets—particularly those markets in developing countries that traded heavily with the United States. Developed markets such as those in western Europe and Japan were less enthusiastic, as they felt they had their own resources and organizations that suited their needs just fine.

The bad news was that, regardless of market, ASQ was perceived to be a very U.S.-centric organization—one in which foreign cultures and language and needs that were different from those in the United States were simply not understood or appreciated. In other words, while there were clear opportunities in overseas markets for ASQ to become more active, no one familiar with ASQ felt it had the institutional culture or structure to be able to do this effectively. Furthermore, while some liked that the "A" in ASQ stood for American, a significant part of the world felt that this label was restrictive and would hinder ASQ's growth in their market beyond the limited sphere of U.S.-based multinational companies that had a presence there.

In effect, ASQ realized that it had two markets abroad: one was the employees and customers of U.S. multinational companies or those companies that otherwise traded with the United States; and the other was employees of indigenous companies that had an interest in quality quite apart from anything to do with the United States. While ASQ might have a quick advantage in penetrating the first market, the second market—which was and is much larger—was inaccessible to them unless they shed themselves of their U.S.-centric structure, identity, and approach.

Following this primary research, ASQ undertook comparative market research using widely available secondary sources for the purpose of identifying the best markets for them to target. The best markets were identified as those that met the following criteria: they were large; they were growing quickly; they had a significant trading relationship with the United States; they were open legally and culturally to penetration by international associations; there were no competing organizations present; and ASQ had already identified potential partners and members that could facilitate their market entry.

Using the results of this tiered research, ASQ identified and prioritized the top four markets that they should have as targets. These markets were China, India, Brazil, and Korea. Mexico and Canada were added to this list because while ASQ already had a sizable presence in those two countries, they were treated operationally and in terms of ASQ governance structures as if they were part of the United States. To the extent ASQ knew it would have to restructure itself to accommodate the global opportunities identified in these four countries, they knew they would have to give special care to ensuring that the same principles also applied to the way ASQ worked with Mexico and Canada.

ASQ's solution was to design operational and governance structures that allowed them to work effectively in the two types of overseas markets that had been identified. In other words, overseas members could continue to have a close relationship to the U.S. side of ASQ if they so wanted; but indigenous markets could opt in favor of a generic ASQ International in which there was no American connection in name or in substance in any aspect of the operations or governance structures.

ASQ staffed up the international part of its operations with multilingual and internationally experienced staff, and it created a separate legal entity—ASQ International—along with a separate international governance body to ensure the direction would remain on track. Finally, three-year business plans were drawn up with budgets and measurable goals for each of the targeted markets.

Two years later, the greatest economic downturn since the Great Depression hit the world's economies. While ASQ's U.S. operations declined significantly with the onset of the recession, this decline was offset by the rapid growth of their international programs. In effect, ASQ has experienced the same phenomenon as almost every global organization—that during times of economic turmoil, those organizations that have the widest market base do best, with global organizations tending to do better than those that are focused on just one national market.

Globalization Is a New Opportunity: Becoming Global Is Not Just for the Wealthy

By 1999, the Project Management Institute (PMI) based in Newtown Square, Pennsylvania, was very much aware that they were sitting on a gold mine. Their project management certification and the related training and testing programs had grown by leaps and bounds since PMI's creation in 1969—with growth particularly acute in the prior three years. One of the key factors in PMI's growth was their success in demonstrating how an organization's performance improved when its personnel were trained and certified in project management. Employees saw project management certification as a career defining and enhancing achievement, and energetically lobbied their employers for support. Once convinced of the usefulness of this certification program, employers (including both for-profit corporations and governmental entities) turned themselves into PMI's marketing arm by requiring that their employees take project management courses and seek project management certification! As many of these organizations had a presence abroad, the need for PMI's programs quickly spread to markets outside the United States. Emerging-market nations, with large infrastructure and information technology (IT) capital projects were also quick to see the value in project management and certification.

PMI's problem in 1999 was how to manage a growth curve that, net of attrition, was in excess of 30 percent a year! They were also concerned about the quantum leap in demand for their products and services from markets outside the United States. Should they open up offices abroad to manage these programs? If so, that would be a very expensive undertaking indeed, and one fraught with risk. Renting office space, buying equipment, and hiring personnel—not to mention the possible need of setting up separate legal entities—are all vastly complicated, time-consuming, and expensive, especially when you are doing this from three to six thousand miles away! So it would seem as if the only choices available to PMI were to borrow enormous amounts of money to set up overseas operations or turn away growth opportunities from outside the United States.

PMI's problem was exceptional. It is not often that an organization is presented with such opportunities—but this spontaneous combustion of market opportunities around the world was highly risky. If PMI failed to handle this problem prudently, it could easily overextend itself and end up collapsing in its own growth.

While PMI's situation may have been exceptional, its solution can serve as a good model for any organization seeking to expand rapidly into markets abroad while minimizing risk. Research showed that PMI did indeed need an on-the-ground presence to administer all its various programs and that this presence needed to be indigenous to the market. In other words, they needed locally recognized legal entities that had the knowledge and ability to quickly ramp up and deliver these programs. PMI's research showed that while PMI's product was unique to every market, there were existing organizations in each with enough overlapping interests that strategic partnerships could be developed in which these organizations could be licensed to deliver PMI's products and services. These agreements would protect PMI's intellectual property while guaranteeing a steady flow of revenue back to headquarters with minimal requirement for any other investment. These revenues would allow PMI to grow its headquarters operations—enabling them to produce new intellectual property as well as to serve a growing base of stakeholders.

These strategic partnerships in the form of licensing agreements proved to be a stroke of genius. Not only did they allow PMI instantaneous access to any market in the world at an affordable cost where they had demand, but they also created whole new revenue streams. In addition to remitting royalties to PMI for the products and services they sold, these strategic partners were also paying PMI licensing fees and as well as fees associated with the materials and training that PMI provided them. In effect, these strategic partners were not only agents for delivering PMI's products and services around the world, they were also customers of new types of products and services that PMI had to develop especially for them.

The PMI example proves that you do not have to have huge financial resources to build a global presence; it also demonstrates that solutions to global problems or opportunities can have useful applications back home in your domestic market. PMI's licensed strategic partners now can be found everywhere around the world, as well as in the United States.

Globalization Is a Tidal Force: Doing Well by Doing Good

As measured by literacy levels, life expectancy, and living standards (as reflected by increases in gross domestic product), humans have dramatically benefitted from cross-border sharing of ideas, and the social and business practices brought to every part of the planet by global programs operated by governments, corporations, and associations.

In saying this, however, I do not mean to echo the "greed is good" line from that iconic 1980s movie *Wall Street*. Cross-border linkages do indeed bring the bad with the good. The factors allowing for the rapid transfers of capital and know-how to developing opportunities around the globe have also led to the global sharing of pain when speculative bubbles pop. Wall Street catches cold and people die of pneumonia a half a globe away. And, of course, the tools of globalization have also been used very effectively by those who would take the world back to the dark ages. Failed states like Afghanistan, Yemen, and Somalia no longer suffer in obscurity as they incubate hatred and extremism.

Using these failed states as launching pads, fanatics have shown that they know how to use the technology of globalization to project their poisons onto innocents around the world.

Globalization is not inherently good, nor is it inherently evil. It is a tidal force. If yours is a seaworthy boat, then the tide is likely to lift you; but if you do not have a seaworthy boat or you have lashed yourself inflexibly to the pier, then you are likely to drown as this tide rises over and around you.

By definition, we *Homo sapiens* have inquiring and organizing minds. We are curious to explore and to know; and once we know, we have an overpowering need to master what we have learned and to organize ourselves accordingly. We change and in turn are changed by the ideas and experiences we encounter. In all of this, associations play a key role as change agents and facilitators. In virtually every membership survey our firm has taken with over 200 associations, the most appreciated aspect of association membership is always "networking." In this regard, people and organizations appreciate the opportunities that associations offer to meet their counterparts from other parts of the world and to exchange ideas. Associations also have the lead role in designing and propagating product and professional standards, which helps facilitate the cross-border movement of products and people. And associations can and do help disseminate knowledge and understanding that fill the gaps left by governments and for-profit corporations.

Globalization Is Outreach: Communities of Common Interest

As the name implies, associations are communities—why shouldn't they be communities on a global scale?

If associations are recognized and accorded tax-exempt status in virtually every nation of the world, it is because the role of associations is recognized for the value it brings to society at large. This fact imposes a considerable challenge to association leaders—that they constantly push the boundaries of what might feel comfortable for them. All associations have constituencies, and in this regard all feel most comfortable working with those names and faces that are nearest and that they see most often. The pull to close ranks and to create an ever-narrower circle of friends and acquaintances is formidable. In effect, every organization is drawn to the familiar, and as they are, they consciously or not erect barriers against the unfamiliar. In so doing, they turn themselves into clubs—a group of members who define themselves as much by who they are as who they are not. Exclusivity is an important part of this picture. But those organizations that give in to this temptation are more than likely betraying the broader, more altruistic visions and missions that called them into existence in the first place. Society does not accord legal and financial advantages to organizations that serve no purpose other than themselves.

If the temptation to define oneself within a national context is great, then how much more so in an international and global context! Each and every one of the U.S.-based associations in the case studies referenced in this book was given the same choice when faced with their various challenges—to circle the wagons and concentrate on their core national constituencies, or to follow their more broadly defined visions and missions into unchartered, global territory. In each case, the volunteer and professional leadership of each association chose the latter option, and in each case this decision propelled their organizations into broader, more dynamic roles on the global stage.

This is not an easy decision to make—some might even consider it foolhardy. In retrospect, we can see that they made the right decision, but at the time it was not so clear. What caused them to take this leap into the unknown? Perhaps there were two reasons—one negative and one positive.

In part it may have been because there are not a lot of success stories of organizations that have followed the nationalistic option. There are, in fact, many examples of organizations that turn away from the rest of the world—none that have produced good results. History contains examples of whole countries that have chosen this option—such as Japan before the Meiji restoration, or China during the Cultural Revolution, or Albania prior to the fall of the Iron Curtain. Organizations, like these countries, that close themselves off to the rest of the world very quickly become anachronistic—irrelevant backwaters in the broader course of human affairs. The option to turn inward buys a limited amount of time perhaps—a temporary fool's paradise—but a dismal end is always in store. In their heart of hearts, most people know this to be true.

In part the decision may have been because these leaders realized that while the global field may be filled with uncertainty, it is also where the future is going to be determined; and it is safer to take on this challenge from the relative safety of an association than it is one member at a time. As noted throughout this book, this is the very legitimate role that associations play in our globalized economy. But we have also seen that a certain kind of enthusiasm for globalization's potential can lead to destructive competition and greed and that this also can undermine attempts to create global organizations.

Doing Well by Doing Good—Continued

International development agencies have known for some time the beneficial role associations can play in helping to develop a country's infrastructure. Those associations that have learned to participate in such programs have most certainly done well by doing good, as virtually every association has that has defined its mission on a global scale. What, in fact, could your organization do if it defined itself as representing the global community? Some might find this thought intimidating or naive; others might find it inspiring. Which of these two groups is most likely to change the world?

There are new challenges (or perhaps old challenges that have been newly recognized?) that national governments and for-profit corporations seem ill-equipped to handle. Pollution, greenhouse gases, and disease do not respect artificial boundaries. Even illiteracy and poverty are seen increasingly to be globally shared problems that have economic and security implications for all of us. Facing such global challenges are a few international structures that were conceived over 60 years ago and many national structures that were conceived many more years ago—none of which have proven entirely up to the task because of the limitations of their perspectives and competencies! In their place, we are increasingly seeing associations and other forms of nonprofit organizations coming forward to address these critical needs. Why shouldn't your association be among them?

About the Author

Steven M. Worth is a management consultant specializing in working with the public sector as well as with for-profit and nonprofit organizations in the diverse fields of education, health care, natural resources, professional services, and workforce development. His specific area of expertise is in addressing the operational and governance opportunities and challenges presented by globalization.

As a consultant and as a business manager himself, Steve has lived and/or designed and managed projects in 110 countries. He has directed or assisted in the creation of the globalization plans of dozens of organizations that have built and run sustainable operations in most all of the world's developed economies as well as many parts of the developing and lesser developed economies.

Steve is president of the Washington, D.C.–based international consulting firm, Plexus Consulting Group, LLC. He has authored over 100 published articles on globalization and a variety of management topics and is the author of *The Power of Partnership* (2008, ASAE & The Center), a book that uses a case-study approach to study the best practices of organizations in forming strategic partnerships.

Worth has an advanced degree from the Sorbonne and l'Ecole des Sciences Politiques in Paris and an undergraduate degree from Georgetown University. He is an adjunct professor of graduate-level courses in international marketing, marketing management, and the marketing of services at Johns Hopkins University.

Index